The Business Process Ecosystem

The Business Process Ecosystem

Arthur C. Harris

Meghan-Kiffer Press
Tampa, Florida, USA, www.mkpress.com
Advanced Business-Technology Books for Competitive Advantage

Related Books from Meghan-Kiffer Press

Business Innovation in the Cloud:
Executing on Innovation with Cloud Computing

Enterprise Cloud Computing:
A Strategy Guide for Business and Technology Professionals

Dot Cloud: The 21st Century Business Platform

Extreme Competition:
Innovation and the Great 21st Century Business Reformation

Samurai Business:
The Way of the Warrior in the Digital Century

The Real-Time Enterprise: Competing on Time

Business Process Management: The Third Wave

Business Process Management: A Rigorous Approach

IT Doesn't Matter—Business Processes Do

Business Process Management: A Practical Guide

Business Process Management is a Team Sport:
Play it to Win!

The Death of 'e' and
the Birth of the Real New Economy

Enterprise E-Commerce

Meghan-Kiffer Press
Tampa, Florida, USA
www.mkpress.com
Advanced Business-Technology Books for Competitive Advantage

Publisher's Cataloging-in-Publication Data

Harris, Arthur C.
The Business Process Ecosystem
p. cm.
Includes bibliographic references and index.
ISBN 10: 0-929652-46-0 ISBN 13: 978-0-929652-46-7 (pbk. : alk paper)
1. Business Process 2. Computer software--Development. 3.
QA76.76.H464 2004   Library of Congress Control Number: 2013932698
005.1 --dc22   CIP

Published by Meghan-Kiffer Press
310 East Fern Street — Suite G
Tampa, FL 33604 USA
Any product mentioned in this book may be a trademark of its company.

Meghan-Kiffer books are available at special quantity discounts for corporate education and training use. For more information write Special Sales, Meghan-Kiffer Press, Suite G, 310 East Fern Street, Tampa, Florida 33604 or email info@mkpress.com

Meghan-Kiffer Press
Tampa, Florida, USA
Publishers of Advanced Business-Technology Books for Competitive Advantage

Printed in the United States of America. SAN 249-7980
MK Printing 10 9 8 7 6 5 4 3 2 1

Acknowledgements

To Jeffrey Gitomer (*Little Red Book of Selling*), who first gave me the idea to write this book.

To Professors Yvonne Antonucci and Penelope (Sue) Greenberg at Widener University who provided their invaluable insights, ideas and comments.

To Brian Hermes, who was kind enough to temporarily come out of retirement to provide guidance in structuring and formatting this book.

To Lesley Stewart who consistently challenged my concepts and thinking.

To Scottie Jacob, Anuradha Potluri and Marilyn Babb of Meghan-Kiffer Press who did a superb job of editing the text.

Table of Contents

Foreword by
Professor Yvonne Antonucci

Business Process Management (BPM) has received much attention in recent years. In fact it seems everyone who has a stake in the BPM arena has chimed in, in one fashion or another. As a result BPM has become a buzz word with little direction. The confusion of what BPM is and what it entails has increased in the halls of organizations across the world. In this book, Arthur Harris pulls together not only what BPM is but more importantly how to do it. His practical approach makes this an easy guide to use to deploy and manage a business process ecosystem. The material in this book is based on the many years of experience Arthur has accumulated working with organizations around the globe who had reached a level of frustration in their business process endeavors. Arthur's talent in BPM is his ability to step in and turn a frustrated and stalled BPM initiative into a successful, productive environment. This book details the success factors and activities Arthur uses to achieve positive results.

Have you wondered why BPM has not taken off in industry? This book addresses this question early on by analyzing what organizations are doing and why. Problems are identified followed by possible causes and effects, followed by feasible solutions to address the problem. A manager could easily use this book as a manual to help identify problems and develop a plan of action to correct them.

This book covers the entire BPM ecosystem from strategy to execution to transformation. It provides a practical approach and explanation of how to build a BPM strategy, how to model organizational processes, and then how to build an infrastructure of BPM elements needed to manage, sustain, and transform organizational business processes. Arthur provides a practical step-by-step approach to each topic, such as how to utilize existing reference models (SCOR, APQC, and so on) to model your organization's processes. He also addresses the need for people, governance, and strategy to sustain the business process ecosystem while maintaining the security and control of organizational processes. He integrates process measurements and KPIs throughout the ecosystem to ensure a continued transformation of the business process ecosystem.

Arthur has a unique method of taking the contributions from several BPM thought leaders and presenting these methods in a clear fashion with the added contribution on how to deploy these methods simply for various situations. Whether you are just starting your BPM journey or you have been working on one for a while, you will find this book useful. It can be used as a guide while you are in the middle of your journey or as a manual to help you launch your BPM initiative successfully. In fact, this book frequently addresses WHY and answers with HOW. This is a must for practitioners of BPM.

Yvonne Antonucci, Ph.D.
Professor, Widener University, PA

Introduction

Business Process Management (BPM) can be described as a discipline dedicated to a process-centric organizational focus, for both operational and strategic activities, with the goal of true integration of management, organizational issues, people, process, and technology.

The reasons for any organization to implement BPM can be best articulated by Mark McGregor, who wrote the following in a article for BPTrends.

To simply talk of improving quality, managing process thinking, changing organizations, or automating existing processes is to miss the real motivation behind BPM. In discussing such topics, we can gain understanding as to why (despite increasing sales) BPM is not truly embedded in our management thinking and our boardrooms. Such topics act like painkillers for a headache and appeal to our sense of reason.

It is not about the cheaper, faster, better paradigm that so many companies are still chasing. It is not about finding new ways to manage staff and monitor activity – such techniques still belong to old style corporate monoliths. It is about bringing together all the assets of a company in a logical catalogued fashion such that they can be broken apart and reassembled in new ways, innovative ways such that our companies can create new products or services and address markets that our competitors have not even thought about yet.

It is about recognizing that knowledge is the key asset in the organization, along with ensuring that the company has the structure and flexibility to bring that knowledge to bear in a quick and focused way to capitalize on an opportunity, and to then be able to dismantle that structure and reassign people and assets when the steam runs out, all the while changing and adapting. [1].

The assets McGregor refers to include people, process, and technology. The development, management and improvement of business processes are a key component of BPM.

There are many books that provide guidance to business process practitioners as to what they should do and the need to develop flow diagrams. There is, however, very little guidance on *how* to start any business process initiative, and more importantly, *how* to develop business processes.

My personal aim is to change the way business processes are developed, and in doing so, enable the flexible enterprise that McGregor describes.

In this book I explain in detail how to start a process initiative as well as how to develop all the business process support constructs, which I call business process support elements. This book assists business executives and process practitioners with two key components of BPM:

(1) *How to define the scope of business processes and subsequent business process design activities.* Before an organization designs its business processes it should understand the complex relationships between policies, procedures, business rules, systems transactions, and data standards. Understanding these complex inter relationships help define the true scope of business processes. I believe that most executives and business process practitioners do not understand the scope of business processes and believe that a business process is the same as a process flow diagram. This is not true. There is a lot more to a business process than a process flow diagram. To this end I have provided the definition of what I call a Business Process Ecosystem, which explains all the elements required for a business process to be properly defined, executed, managed, measured and optimized.

(2) *How to develop business processes and all their supporting constructs.* The objectives of this book are to provide:

- An easy to read guide to business executives that details *why* their processes are important and *how* they can do a better job of defining these processes.
- An alternative approach to business process definition by providing new tools and concepts to business process analysts to do business process design and development: a *different, better, and*

faster way.

- The starting point for moving an organization to a business process mindset and assist management in starting the journey.
- A view of what the end product of a business process definition exercise could look like. To answer the question: *"What does 'done' look like?"*
- Provide executives the path forward to do business process development in a structured and complete way so that the organization's business processes become an asset.

Structure of this book

This book has been structured and written in such a way that it can be easily read and referenced. It's divided into five sections:

- Section one grounds the reader in basic business process fundamentals, and thus serves as a baseline for the rest of the book.
- Section two introduces the reader to the concept of a Business Process Ecosystem, and its components.
- Section three assists readers in identifying and defining requirements for the business process ecosystem. The section also describes selling and educating the organization on the value of developing an ecosystem, and provides readers with preparation activities that should be completed before commencing the development of the ecosystem.
- Section four covers the development of key ecosystem components, including the business process decomposition model.
- Section five describes the business process support elements, how to develop them, and the benefits of developing them.

Section One: The Basics

The first section of this book contains brief chapters devoted to each of the following four basic questions.

- *What is a business process?* A clear and concise definition of a business process shows readers that a process must have a purpose and must also deliver results. There is no point in having a business process that either provides no results, or has no clear purpose.

- *What types of business processes are there?* Why is it important to know this? Most organizations focus on operations processes and spend little or no time focusing on management processes, or on the processes that differentiate them. Understanding that there are different types of processes allows you to focus on the processes that are really important.

- *Why are business processes important?* Organizations manage their employees who execute business processes, and manage the outputs of these processes. Everything we do in an organization is done through the execution of business processes. Does management really believe business processes are important? Or should we be asking the question "how can processes not be important?"

- *Why is the adoption of business process management so hard?* What are the roadblocks to implementing BPM and why are organizations not doing it?

Notes and Action Items

1. What is a Business Process?

Before discussing a Business Process Ecosystem and what it consists of, it makes sense to provide a definition of what a business process is. The best and most complete definition, and explanation of a business process I have found, is the one by Michael Hammer. [2]

"A process is 'an organized group of related activities that together create a result of value to customers.' Each word in this definition is important:

- A process is a *group* of activities, not just one. Value is created not by single activities, but by the entire process in which all these tasks merge in a systematic way for a clear purpose.
- Activities are *related* and *organized*. They present a stream of relevant, interconnected activities that must be performed in sequence – the right things in the right way – to produce the desired outcome.
- All the activities in the process work *together* toward a common goal. 'People performing different steps of a process must all be aligned around a single purpose, instead of focusing on their individual tasks in isolation.'
- Processes are not ends in themselves. They have a purpose; they create and deliver results that customers care about."

To the above I would add: Processes are best identified in the "Verb Noun" format: (for example, "Plan Shipments" – Plan being the verb). Processes are best described in terms of what is being done, without regard to who is doing the activity, which business function does the activity, or where it is done.

Roger Maull, Director of the Exeter University Centre for Research in Strategic Processes & Operations, defines the essential characteristics of processes as follows [3]:

- Processes have customers, internal and external.
- Processes are independent of formal organizational structure.
- Processes may cross organizational boundaries.

- Processes should be linked to strategic objectives.

The above characteristics are worth looking at a little deeper, since they further assist in the definition of a business process:

- A business process has customers (internal or external). A business process must serve a purpose, otherwise it is not needed.
- Processes are independent of an organization. Processes are about work being done, not where the work is done. Business processes should not be confused with an organization chart.
- Processes may cross organizational boundaries. They are not limited to only your organization. An organization that manages inventory for its customers, at the customer's site, is an example of a cross-organizational process.
- Processes should be linked to strategy, because an organization's strategies are enabled through its processes.

2. Types of Business Processes

Business processes can typically be categorized in the following groupings.

Management Processes

Management processes are processes that are executed by management. These processes can be further classified into 2 types:

1) *Processes that managers perform in running the business.*
   Processes that allow managers to develop strategies do business planning, and perform budgeting activities are examples of these processes.

2) *Processes that govern the work that gets done by the operational processes.* These processes could include processes that sales management would follow to manage the business of sales, such as the processes that track sales orders and monitor for potential delays in delivering products to customers. These processes are typically overlooked during ERP implementations or process optimization initiatives.

Core Processes

Strategic or core processes (strategic to your business), are typically defined as processes that create value for an organization. An organization that manufactures goods, for example, would classify its manufacturing processes as core or strategic.

Support Processes

Support processes are typically defined as being non-core processes and are not strategic in nature. In a manufacturing organization, processes for finance (perform revenue accounting) and human resources (recruit and retain employees) are not core processes.

A process can also be a core process in one industry and be a support process in another industry. For example, in the Aerospace and Defense Industry, procurement processes are seen as being core, whereas in an industry such as Higher Education, procurement is seen as a support process.

Enabling Processes

Enabling Processes are those processes that enable and maintain the core or support processes. The Supply Chain Council's SCOR Model [4], consists of "enabling processes." Enabling processes are discussed in more detail in Chapter 10.

Most firms focus on the core processes when it comes to implementing ERP or doing process improvement initiatives. The support or enabling processes are seen as being secondary or are forgotten.

A good example of an enabling process is the *Develop & Manage Pricing* process. This process contains the tasks that define and manage an organization's pricing activities. These processes are important in the development and management of changes in product and service pricing. The Sales Order process (a core process) uses the results of this process (the pricing conditions) to price a customer order. If this process was not developed then the sales order process could not price a sales order. Any organization that bundles products and services or has highly engineered products would agree that the *Develop and Manage Pricing* process is complex.

Developing these processes would make an organization more effective, plus the "low hanging fruit" in any process optimization initiative can be found in optimizing the enabling processes.

In Summary

The classification or allocation of a process to a particular process category is not that important. What is important, however, is that processes are not omitted or forgotten during process definition efforts, and that all processes are identified and developed.

All processes are important. For example, an organization's accounts payable processes may not be strategic, but when vendors refuse to deliver product because of prior nonpayment, a core process such as manufacturing could be affected. No matter what type of process it is, a poorly developed process results in rework, inefficiencies, and employee frustration.

While the above categorization of processes is comprehensive, there are three additional representations of an organization's business processes:

- Processes that assist in differentiating an organization's products and services and that provide strategic advantage over its competitors,
- Processes that are structured or unstructured, and
- Processes that are customer focused (external) versus internally focused.

Processes that Provide Competitive Advantage

These are the processes that an organization excels in and provides strategic advantage to the organization. Let us use Apple Inc. as an example. Apple is a company that is seen as being highly innovative and has developed market leading products such as the iPod, iPhone and the iPad. Apple's ideation processes (idea development) are the processes used to develop ideas and products. These are the processes that allow them to differentiate themselves from the company's competitors.

Apple's payroll processes or financial processes, on the other hand, can be described as being non-strategic.

An organization needs to understand which of its processes provide strategic differentiation and should then focus and spend the time measuring and optimizing these processes.

For non-strategic processes, organizations would be best served by adopting industry best practices and should not spend any time trying to differentiate these processes. To quote Lou Farina, the head of Master Data Management at Colgate Palmolive, who was talking in the context of the company's processes that create and manage master data: "There is no strategic advantage to Colgate to create vendors in a non-standard way."

Structured vs. Unstructured Processes

Unstructured processes are those processes that are typically iterative in nature or whose activities cannot be controlled. An example of an unstructured process is a sales process. A company has no control over a customer's buying process, and as a result, most sales cycles are unique to the customer. Other examples include Product Prototyping, and Drug Research processes. These processes are unstructured because it is very difficult to estimate task durations, sequences, etc. Activities can be repeated and take longer or shorter depending on a given situation.

For unstructured processes, don't spend too much time and effort trying to structure them; time would best be spent developing tools to facilitate or support these processes.

Structured processes are those processes whose activities can be predicted, modeled, and controlled. An example of a structured process is a payroll processing process. Time should be spent developing, managing, and optimizing these processes.

Internal vs. External Processes

External or outward facing processes are those that affect or require interaction with suppliers, customers and other business partners. External processes expose an organization to external entities. If these processes are poorly executed, an organization's customers and other business partners will have a poor impression of the organization. Any process that affects your customer is more important than those processes that do not touch your customer. As a rule, customer-facing processes are the most important. Processes that support sales and customer service are examples of these types of processes.

It could be argued that internal or inward facing processes are less important than external processes. Processes that support the Human Resources and Finance business functions are two examples of internal processes that do not interact with customers. As a rule, an organization should spend more time optimizing outward facing processes than inward facing processes. It makes sense to stress that while all processes in an organization are important, external facing processes are more visible and thus more important.

Reasons for Categorizing Business Processes

Categorizing business processes ensures that an organization:

- Does not forget to develop any processes, and it develops processes in all the categories of processes.
- Focuses on the processes that are important: core, differentiated, and customer-facing processes.
- Focuses on adopting Best Practices or industry standards for those processes that do not need to be differentiated.
- Allows the organization to prioritize technology and process improvement projects, based on the importance of the processes to the business.

Notes and Action Items

3. Why Business Processes are Important

Everything an organization does is through the execution of structured or unstructured business processes. Business processes are about work and how work gets done in an organization. The Oxford dictionary definition of *work* is "activity involving mental or physical effort done in order to achieve a result."

Work is done in an organization by following a series of predefined steps or activities. These predefined steps or activities are called business processes. All work is thus done through the execution of business processes.

- Strategies and plans are developed through planning processes.
- Products and services are developed through a design process.
- Goods are manufactured by following manufacturing processes.
- Customers are supported by customer service processes.
- Employees are managed by human capital management processes.

This is why business processes are important.

We live in a world of rapid product commoditization and explosive growth of emerging markets and countries such as Brazil, Russia, India and China (BRIC). The experts all agree that competing in a global economy involves product innovation, maximizing growth in existing markets, and opening new markets. However, the way a company does its business is the key to sustaining competitive advantage. It is no longer simply enough to do what you do, it is how you do it that matters, and those are your business processes. [4] Following are comments from thought leaders that provide answers to the question, "Why are business processes important?"

Extreme Competition

Peter Fingar is an internationally recognized expert on business strategy, globalization and business process management. As a practitioner with over thirty years of hands-on experience at the intersection of business and technology, he makes the case for organizations to make deep structural changes in the ways they operate their businesses. Fingar provides insight into 13 strategies a company must embrace to compete going forward. Extreme Business Processes represents one of these 13 strategies:

"So, what strikes fear in the hearts of business leaders these days? Globalization and commoditization. We are not on the brink of a new world economic order; we've already crossed that threshold. With three billion new capitalists from China, India and the former Soviet Union ready to engage your company in extreme competition, you'll have to make deep structural changes in the very ways you operate your business, the very ways you do what you do—and that's what Extreme Competition is all about. Operational innovation—where you forge new relationships across the globe to form extreme supply chains, pursue extreme innovation and collaborate with extreme specialists—is the next true source of competitive advantage." [4] (See back matter for *Extreme Competition*.)

Balanced Scorecard and Strategy Maps

Business Strategy is based on a differentiated customer value proposition. Satisfying customers is the source of sustainable value creation. Strategy requires a clear articulation of targeted customer segments and the value proposition required to please them. Clarity of this value proposition is the single most important dimension of strategy. [5]

Value is created through internal business processes. The financial and customer perspectives in strategy maps and balanced scorecards describe the outcomes (i.e., what the organization hopes to achieve); increases in shareholder value through revenue growth and productivity improvements; and increases in the company's share of customer spending through customer acquisition, satisfaction, retention, loyalty, and growth.

Processes drive strategy; they describe how the organization will implement its strategy. Effective and aligned internal processes determine how value gets created and sustained. Companies must focus on the critical few internal processes that deliver the differentiating value proposition and that are most critical for enhancing productivity and maintaining the organization's franchise to operate. The internal processes are classified into four clusters:

- *Operations management:* Producing and delivering products and services to customers.
- *Customer management:* Establishing and leveraging relationships with customers.
- *Innovation:* Developing new products, services, processes and relationships.
- *Regulatory and social:* Conforming to regulations and societal expectations and building stronger communities.

Competitive Strategy

Michael Hammer, the famed leader in business strategy quoted: "Competitive strategy is about being different. It means deliberately choosing a different set of activities to deliver a unique mix of value. The essence of strategy is in the activities, choosing to perform activities differently or to perform different activities than rivals, otherwise, a strategy is nothing more than a marketing slogan that will not withstand competition."[2]

Operational Effectiveness

Operational effectiveness and strategic positioning are both essential approaches to superior performance, which, after all, is the primary goal of any enterprise. These two approaches, however, work in very different ways.

Operational effectiveness means performing similar activities better than rivals perform them. Operational effectiveness includes but is not limited to efficiency. It refers to any number of practices that allow a company to better utilize its inputs by, for example, reducing defects in products or developing better products faster. In contrast, *strategic positioning means performing different activities from rivals or performing similar activities in different ways.* [6]

Notes and Action Items

4. The Challenge of Business Process Management: Why is Adoption So Hard?

During a business school course taught at Widener University (Introduction to Business Process Management), the students were asked the following question: "If everyone understands the importance of business processes, then why are so many organizations not following a formal BPM approach?" The students came up with the following list of reasons:

- Organizations (management in particular) are resistant to change.
- Most businesses are too busy running around putting out fires. They have little time to think and act strategically.
- Someone in the management team has had a prior bad experience in business process management and discourages any talk about processes.
- The functional views in the business are too entrenched, political islands and fiefdoms are the norm.
- Functional managers believe business process management is a danger to the status quo.
- Management is inexperienced and does not have the capabilities to lead the organization to doing things differently.

The reasons the students list are valid yet not comprehensive. Some additional factors that make adopting a formal approach to BPM more difficult are:

- Most executives do not understand the value of managing the business from a business process perspective.
- Management feels they already have their business processes under control.
- Management continues to focus on other activities.

Executives Value Functions over Processes

Most executives do not understand the value of a process perspective to managing the business. Businesses are traditionally setup and run from a functional perspective; where employees are assigned to departments, or business functions, and work within those functions. This organization setup provides focus on the division of tasks and responsibilities within the business functions.

While the Functions Perspective is an accurate and common way of thinking, there is another, more effective, approach to managing an organization: as a series and combination of interacting processes. This approach to managing the business, from a Process Perspective, adds value to an organization in the following ways:

- Provides an overview of how processes are executed throughout the organization.
- Provides insights into the interrelationships and integration points of individual functions and departments.
- Provides a clear view of the integration points and handoffs, thus making these manageable.

Management Relies on the False Assessment that Business Processes are Under Control

Companies often feel they already have their business processes under control. There is a belief in most organizations that if employees are engaged in processing orders, manufacturing goods, and shipping products, then the company's business processes work. This thinking implies that:

- Everyone knows who is doing what work.
- The work is done correctly.
- The work is done efficiently and effectively.
- The quality and timeliness of the work meets the requirements of not only customers, but also that of management.

However, the above thinking is flawed. Business process maturity assessments performed in many different organizations provide a different perspective:

- Management often thinks employees know what to do, who is responsible for what, and assume that employees are generally doing a good job.
- Employees however have a different perspective, they feel they are poorly trained, that processes are not defined and documented, and who is responsible for doing what work is also not clear.

Management Continues to Focus on Other Activities

Companies feel they would be better served by focusing on functional activities other than their business processes.

Very often management in organizations feel they would be better served by focusing their efforts and budget on activities deemed more important than business processes; activities such as sales or product development. In many organizations the lack of sales is often attributed to a lack of competent sales people, or the lack of new products.

Reorganizing the business or hiring new sales people however does not necessarily translate into additional sales, especially if the organization's sales problems are not people related.

Focusing instead on the customer and customer-facing business processes could provide more value to the organization, as happy customers pay quicker, and buy more goods and services.

Many companies do not know where to start. The reason for this is the "M" in BPM. That is to say BPM is a strategic management issue; not a tweaking of individual functional activities. Leadership is all when it comes to adopting strategic BPM.

For an interesting discussion of 21st century business leadership, reference Ken Thompson's book *Bioteams: High Performance Teams Based on Nature's Most Successful Designs*. Ken takes you on a fascinating journey from command-and-control to connect-and-collaborate leadership where every member of the executive team is a leader. (See back matter for information on Thompson's book.)

Section Two: The Business Process Ecosystem

Section two of this book introduces and explains the concept and components of a business process ecosystem.

The business process ecosystem introduces the concept that the design and development of business processes should consist of all the objects that form the complex relationships between processes, policies, procedures, business rules, systems transactions, and data.

The introduction to the business process ecosystem is completed by introducing business process support elements. Business process support elements are all the objects that allow a process to be executed, measured, managed, and optimized.

Chapter 5 introduces readers to the business process ecosystem, and describes the components of the ecosystem.

Chapter 6 explains the core or central construct of the business process ecosystem, the business process decomposition model.

Notes and Action Items

5. Business Process Ecosystems

Most people think of process flow diagrams when a business process is mentioned or discussed. There is, however, a lot more to a business process than a flow diagram. The design and development of business processes should consist of all the objects that form the complex relationships between processes, policies, procedures, business rules, systems transactions, and data.

Developing process flow diagrams only during business process design initiatives allows for incomplete business process development. Understanding the components of the ecosystem allows for the correct scoping and sizing of business process initiatives.

Introduction

Webster's Dictionary defines an *ecosystem* as the complex of a community of organisms and its environment functioning as an ecological unit.

A *business process ecosystem* refers to the collection of processes and all the components that constitute and govern the behavior of business processes and allow processes to be defined, executed, managed, measured, and optimized. The Business Process Ecosystem is centered on "work" and defines:

- The work to be done.
- Who should do the work and how (which role).
- How to manage and control the work from a regulatory and compliance perspective as well as a management controls perspective.
- How work integrates with enablers such as technology.

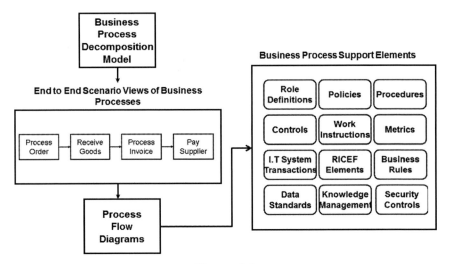

Figure 5.1

The business process ecosystem consists of a number of interrelated components.

- A business process decomposition model
- End to End views of business processes (scenarios)
- Process flow diagrams
- Business process support elements

Business Process Decomposition Model

The Business Process Decomposition Model is a decomposition of all the business processes of an organization. The model includes the core processes of a business, its support processes, and its control processes. A decomposition model can be five, sometimes six or seven levels deep (depending on the intended use of the decomposition model).

Figure 5.2 shows a four-level process decomposition model for the "deliver products and services" processes.

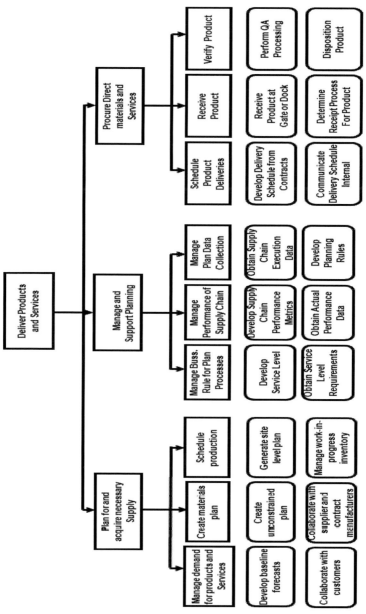

Figure 5.2

Scenario Views of the Business Process Decomposition Model

Scenario views are best described as end-to-end business processes. These end-to-end processes consist of a series of business processes that are strung together, or combined to describe a complete end-to-end scenario.

An example of a scenario is "Quote to Cash." This scenario includes all quotation, sales, delivery, and receivables processes.

Process teams, process owners, or supply chain managers can create different views of the model for themselves; either as a subset of Level 1 processes, or to combine processes across Level 2 processes. Some examples of this could be:

- Developing a "Plan to Receive" scenario by combining plan processes with procurement processes as well as the manage in-bound logistics processes.
- Developing a "Plan to Make" scenario by combining plan processes with manufacturing processes.
- Developing an "Order to Install" scenario by combining sales order processes with engineering processes and installation processes.

End-to-end scenarios should be defined once the process decomposition model is completed. This will allow for the easy definition of which processes the scenario consists of. This activity will be easily facilitated if the process decomposition model is documented and stored in a process repository for future access.

Process Flow Diagrams

A process flow diagram is a graphical view of a business process. It consists of tasks or activities and shows sequencing, inputs, outputs, and decision points. A process flow diagram can be drawn for any process, and at any level within the business process decomposition model.

Figure 5.3 below shows a simple process flow diagram.

Create and Approve Purchase Requisitions

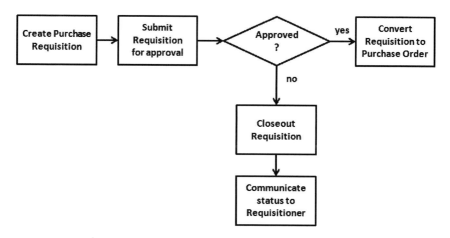

Figure 5.3

Business Process Support Elements

Business Process Support Elements are the constructs required for a process to be defined, managed, measured, optimized, and executed. Below is a list of business process support elements.

- Role Descriptions
- Systems Security Controls
- Policies
- Procedures
- Business Rules
- Metrics and Key Performance Indicators (KPI's)
- Work Instructions
- System Transactions
- Data Standards
- Controls
- Reports, Interfaces, Conversions, Extracts and Forms (RICEF elements)
- Knowledge management and organizational learning content

Business Process Support Elements can best be explained by following a returns business process. Employees who work in the goods receiving department need to understand how to execute the returns activity. Employees need to be trained to do the work and provided task level instructions that will guide them through the activity. We will call these instructions Work Instructions.

The employees need to understand the rules or guidelines of the process (i.e., "Can I accept a return good for an item that is out of warranty?"). Business rules must be developed so that when an employee experiences a decision point (such as the one above), the employee knows how to react. These business rules must be documented and disseminated.

In this returns example, the policy must also be made available to customers. A procedure must be developed for customers explaining how and by when to return the products.

If the returns process is supported by a computer system, the person executing the system transaction needs to have the correct authorization levels to execute the transaction. The person entering the system transaction also needs to understand how to execute the transaction and what data to enter into the screens. Role based system security profiles, system transaction documentation, and data standards need to be developed to facilitate the execution of system transactions.

From the above example readers can see that a process cannot exist by itself. It needs all the business process support elements to be in place so that the process can be developed completely, maintained, enhanced, managed, and supported.

6. The Business Process Decomposition Model

The Business Process decomposition model is the core construct of the Business Process Ecosystem. As stated earlier, the Business Process Decomposition Model is a hierarchical decomposition of all the processes within an organization. It is also sometimes referred to as a Process Framework. Semantics aside, what this is, is a model of business processes. Note that this is not a functional view, but a view of the processes within the business.

Developing a Business Process Decomposition Model should be the first step in any business process endeavor as it provides a structure that facilitates the identifying of all business processes. It also provides the data required to scope and resource any process project, as processes can be counted and the development effort can be estimated. The Business Process Decomposition Model is the foundation of the Business Process Ecosystem because:

- It allows for identifying *all* the business processes within an organization. Building a Decomposition Model allows for the identification of not only the core processes, but also the Enable, Control, and Governance processes.
- It allows for identifying integration points between different processes because the model allows multiple processes to be seen at the same time.
- It provides an enterprise-wide view of all processes and as such is the roadmap for all business processes within an organization.
- It provides a structure to develop and define end-to-end processes and scenarios because the model structure allows for the combining of multiple processes.
- It provides a structure to identify, develop, and associate the Business Process Support Elements with any level within the Decomposition Model.

The Business Process Decomposition Model is not:

- A functional view of a business (i.e. HR, Manufacturing, or Finance), but rather a process view of a business.
- A chart showing the importance of processes in a hierarchy.
- An organization chart.

Section Three: Preparation Activities

This section covers both learning activities and project preparation activities that are necessary to complete the development of the business process ecosystem.

Defining the scope of the business process ecosystem is important before commencing its development. This will require some education of the organization (management included) on what the process ecosystem is, and its potential applications within the organization. This will assist in the definition of requirements and the scoping of the ecosystem.

Chapter 7 covers education activities that must be performed to facilitate the adoption and development of the business process ecosystem.

Chapter 8 reviews regulations an organization may need to comply with, and how these regulations can result in the development of business process support elements.

Chapter 9 provides readers into existing industry models that are available. The models are explained, and their strengths and weaknesses are reviewed. Understanding the business process decomposition model, what it is, and how it could be used is important, as it is a critical component of the business process ecosystem. A key preparation activity is to review existing process decomposition models. It is not necessary to develop a business process decomposition model from scratch, as there are numerous models available that can be used as a starting point.

Chapter 10 reviews the differences between business processes and business functions. Business process development is often sub-optimized when business functions and business processes are viewed inter-changeably. Understanding the differences between processes and functions will prevent this sub-optimization.

Chapter 11 provides activities to develop goals and requirements of the ecosystem. This step is important to not only get organization buy-in, but the requirements will help define the scope of the ecosystem.

Chapter 12 covers the activities to finalize the scope of the Business Process Ecosystem.

Chapter 13 covers the definition of goals and objectives of the business process decomposition model. This step will help determine the number of levels in the model.

Chapter 14 introduces readers to process decomposition level terminology of existing models, and allows readers to define their own level terminology or naming conventions.

Chapter 15 reviews requirements from a technology perspective to support the business process ecosystem. The use of a technology will facilitate the management of the process ecosystem.

We will approach the development of the Business Process Ecosystem as a project. The approach to developing the Business Process Ecosystem is mapped below.

Project Startup
- Setup Team

Preparation and Education Activities
- Setup project team
- Educate the organization
- Understand the regulations with which your organization needs to comply
- Analyze and understand existing Industry models
- Understand the difference between processes and functions
- End-to-end scenarios
- Define a model structure
- Identify and select terminology
- Define goals and requirements of ecosystem
- Define scope of the Business Process Ecosystem
- Define goals and objectives of the process decomposition model

Develop the Business Process Ecosystem
- Develop or extend the Business Process Decomposition Model
- Develop end-to-end scenarios

Develop Business Process Support Elements
- Develop process flow diagrams
- Develop work instructions
- Develop role definitions
- Develop system security controls
- Business rules
- Policies
- Procedures
- Systems transactions
- Data standards
- Business and process controls
- Metrics
- Reports, Interfaces, Conversions, Extensions, and Forms (RICEF)
- Knowledge management

Notes and Action Items

7. Educate the Organization

It is important to educate the organization on what a business process ecosystem is, what its applications could be, and what the benefits to the organization would be. The adoption, development, and continued support of the ecosystem require organizational buy-in and commitment. It is important to state here that the BPE is a tool for the business, and thus belongs to the business.

It is virtually impossible to define meaningful goals and objectives, and gather requirements to scope the ecosystem, if the organization is not educated. Education efforts should include:

The Business Process Ecosystem
- Explain the components of the ecosystem.
- Describe applications of the ecosystem within the organization.
- Describe the benefits of developing a business process ecosystem.
- Describe how not developing it effects the organization today.

The Business Process Decomposition Model
- Use the APQC Decomposition Model as an example to explain what a Decomposition Model is. The APQC model is explained in Chapter 9.
- Describe applications within the organization.
- Describe the benefits of developing a Business Process Decomposition Model.

Business Process Support Elements
- Explain each Business Process Support Element.
- Describe the uses of the Business Process Support Elements.
- Describe the benefits of developing each Business Process Support Element.
- Use the example in the appendix to explain the role that each Business Process Support Element plays in the support of business processes.

Notes and Action Items

8. Understand the Regulations Affecting Your Organization

Most organizations have to comply with regulations. If an organization is in a highly regulated industry such as Pharmaceutical or Nuclear Energy, it has many regulations it needs to comply with.

Many regulations have the sole purpose of ensuring that organizations have proper controls in place. For instance, the Health Information Privacy Assurance Act (HIPAA) requires that proper controls over information security and privacy are in place to protect patient records. Sarbanes-Oxley (SOX) demands that publicly traded companies in the United States use controls to ensure that their financial statements are accurate.

A Pharmaceutical company that is publicly traded, that develops drugs for human consumption needs to comply with:

- Federal Drug Administration (FDA) Guidelines
- International Conference on Harmonization (ICH) Good Clinical Practices (GCP) Guidelines
- Good Manufacturing Practice (GMP)
- Good Laboratory Practices (GLP)
- Health Information Privacy Assurance Act (HIPAA)
- Sarbanes Oxley (SOX)

It is important to review the regulations that your organization needs to comply with when developing a Business Process Ecosystem, because the compliance of these regulations will result in the development of one or more ecosystem elements.

The ICH guideline 3.1.8 explains the responsibilities of the Institutional Review Board (IRB) as follows: The IRB/IEC should review both the amount and method of payment to subjects to assure that neither presents problems of coercion or undue influence on the trial

51

subjects. Payments to a subject should be prorated and not wholly contingent on completion of the trial by the subject.

The actions the organization takes to comply with ICH Guideline 3.1.8 may include the following Business Processes, and Business Process Support Elements. Business processes could include:

- Processes for an IRB to review, agree, or reject payments.
- Processes to review and maintain payment limit rules.
- Processes to review and maintain payment proration rules.

Business process support elements could include:

- Business Rules describing payment limits.
- Business Rules describing payment proration rules.
- Controls to monitor that proration payments are in compliance with proration rules.
- Role Descriptions for reviewing and maintaining business rules.
- Systems Transactions that disburse prorated payments.

From the above, you can understand why it is important to review your organization's regulations; this activity will help you identify business process support elements that must be developed, and ensure the completeness of your business processes.

To support GMP (Good Manufacturing Practices) we will use GMP 211.22 as an example to develop a spreadsheet with the following columns:

- Column 1 – Regulation number: 211.22
- Column 2 – Regulation group: Responsibilities of quality control unit.
- Column 3 – Regulation Description: There shall be a quality control unit that shall have the responsibility and authority to approve or reject all components, drug product containers, closures, in-process materials, packaging material, labeling, and drug products, and the authority to review production records to assure that no errors have occurred or, if errors have occurred, that they have been fully investigated. The quality control unit shall be responsible for approving or

rejecting drug products manufactured, processed, packed, or held under contract by another company.

- Column 4 – Process: setup processes to QA items
- Column 5 – Rules: develop rules for accept/reject items
- Column 6 - Role: develop role definitions for quality team

Create columns for all process support elements, and add content accordingly. This will allow you support your regulations, as well as ensure your process ecosystem is complete.

Notes and Action Items

9. Analyze and Understand Existing Industry Decomposition Models

There is no reason to develop a Business Process Decomposition Model from scratch. Included in this section are descriptions and features of some existing Industry Decomposition Models or Process Frameworks. Their strengths and their weaknesses are also reviewed. It is recommended that an organization selects the model structure that best fits its needs and creates its own model beginning with that template. Selected processes from the different models can also be incorporated to build an organization specific model.

A key decision to make here is how many levels deep the decomposition model needs to be. This will depend on the requirements that have been gathered earlier. As a point of reference, the Supply Chain Council provides a SCOR Model Overview that provides a justification for a six level decomposition model.

Below is a listing of available industry decomposition models:
- Supply Chain Operations Reference (SCOR) Model
- Design Chain Operations Reference (DCOR) Model
- Customer Chain Operations Reference (CCOR) Model
- Enhanced Telecom Operations Map ("eTOM")
- American Production Quality Control (APQC)

SCOR Model

The SCOR Model is the product of the Supply Chain Council (SCC), an independent, not-for-profit, global corporation with membership open to all companies and organizations interested in applying and advancing the state-of-the-art in supply-chain management systems and practices. [7]

The SCOR Model provides a unique framework that links business processes, metrics, best practices, and technology features into a unified structure to support communication among supply chain partners and to improve the effectiveness of supply chain management and related supply chain improvement activities.

The SCOR Model is a Supply Chain Reference Model and covers the core supply chain processes: Plan, Source, Make, Deliver, and Return. The SCOR model decomposes to three levels of detail. See Figure 9.1 for a graphic that explains the SCOR Model.

Distinguishing Features of the SCOR model include:

- It covers the supply chain processes for Plan, Source, Make, Deliver and Return.
- It contains best practices and metrics; none of the other models contain these.
- The model has a scenario view or a process variant view of key processes, and shows variants of the same process; processes such as Make to Order, Engineer to Order, and Make to Stock are make or manufacturing variants.
- The model contains enabling processes, the support processes that are required to make the core processes work. Other decomposition models either have these enabling processes embedded in other processes or do not have them at all.
- The Model follows an end-to-end process view, across business functions. An example of this is the Procure to Stock process (Source MTS). This process starts with the definition of requirements and ends with the authorizing of supplier payments. This process decomposes to the following five sub processes:
    1. Schedule product deliveries
    2. Receive product
    3. Verify product
    4. Transfer product
    5. Authorize supplier payment

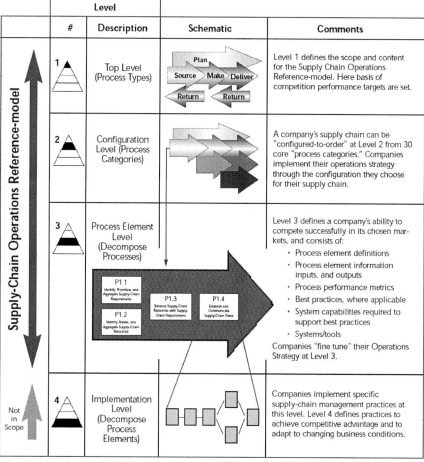

	Level			
	#	Description	Schematic	Comments
Supply-Chain Operations Reference-model	1	Top Level (Process Types)	Plan / Source / Make / Deliver / Return / Return	Level 1 defines the scope and content for the Supply Chain Operations Reference-model. Here basis of competition performance targets are set.
	2	Configuration Level (Process Categories)		A company's supply chain can be "configured-to-order" at Level 2 from 30 core "process categories." Companies implement their operations strategy through the configuration they choose for their supply chain.
	3	Process Element Level (Decompose Processes)	P1.1 Identify, Prioritize, and Aggregate Supply-Chain Requirements / P1.2 Identify, Assess, and Aggregate Supply-Chain Resources / P1.3 Balance Supply-Chain Resources with Supply-Chain Requirements / P1.4 Establish and Communicate Supply-Chain Plans	Level 3 defines a company's ability to compete successfully in its chosen markets, and consists of: • Process element definitions • Process element information inputs, and outputs • Process performance metrics • Best practices, where applicable • System capabilities required to support best practices • Systems/tools Companies "fine tune" their Operations Strategy at Level 3.
Not in Scope	4	Implementation Level (Decompose Process Elements)		Companies implement specific supply-chain management practices at this level. Level 4 defines practices to achieve competitive advantage and to adapt to changing business conditions.

Figure 9.1

What are the gaps in the SCOR model? The model is limited to supply chain processes and therefore does not contain non-supply chain processes such as human resource management, sales order management or any financial processes.

Access to the SCOR model can be obtained by becoming a member of the SCC. Information about the SCOR Model can be obtained from the SCC at www.supply-chain.org.

DCOR Model

The DCOR Model was developed by the business process management organization of Hewlett-Packard (HP). The model's structure was inspired by that of the SCOR Model and follows its design. The DCOR model decomposes to three levels of detail. The Design Chain domain is defined as the collection of business activities associated with all phases of product engineering (R&D):

- The DCOR Model covers the Design Chain processes for Plan, Research, Design, Integrate, and Amend.
- The Model has a scenario view or a process variant view of key processes, and shows variants of the same process. Processes such as Develop New Product, Develop New Technology, and Refresh Product are design variants.
- The model contains enabling processes. These enabling processes are the support processes that are required to make the core processes work. Other decomposition models either have these enabling processes embedded in other processes or do not have them at all. The Model follows an end-to-end process view, across business functions. An example of this is the Research Product Refresh process. This process decomposes to the following five process steps:
    1. Schedule Research Activities
    2. Source Materials
    3. Verify Materials
    4. Transfer Findings and Materials
    5. Authorize Supplier Payment

What are the gaps in the DCOR model? The model is limited to design chain processes and therefore does not contain processes such as Human Resource Management, Sales Order Management, or any Finance processes.

Access to the DCOR Model can be obtained by becoming a member of the SCC. Information about the DCOR Model can be obtained from the SCC at www.supply-chain.org.

CCOR Model

The CCOR Model (Customer Chain Operations Reference Model) was developed by the business process management organization of Hewlett-Packard. The model's structure was inspired by that of the SCOR model and follows its design. The Customer Chain domain is defined as the collection of business activities associated with all phases of converting customer (segments) into orders. The CCOR model decomposes to three levels of detail:

- The CCOR model covers the Customer Chain processes for Plan, Market, Relate, Sell, Contract, and Assist.
- The model has a scenario view or a process variant view of key processes and shows variants of the same process; processes such as Sell to Intermediary, Sell to Grouped Account, and Sell to Named Account are sales variants.
- The model contains enabling processes which are the support processes that are required to make the core processes work.

Other decomposition models either have these enabling processes embedded in other processes or do not have them at all. The Model follows an end-to-end process view, across business functions. An example of this is the Sell to Grouped Account process. This process decomposes to the following five process steps:

1. Select Engagement Model
2. Obtain Customer Needs
3. Determine Proposed Solutions
4. Present Solutions to Customers
5. Release to Contract

What are the gaps in the CCOR Model? The model is limited to customer chain processes and therefore does not contain non-customer chain processes such as human resource management, supply chain management or any financial processes.

Access to the CCOR Model can be obtained by becoming a member of the SCC: supply-chain.org.

Enhanced Telecom Operations Map (eTOM)

The Telemanagement Forum (TM Forum) has developed an Enhanced Telecom Operations Map (eTOM) for the Information and Communications Services Industry. At its most basic, eTOM is a blueprint for telecom companies to implement enterprise practices. Topics are generally broken down into three groups:

- *Strategy, Infrastructure, and Product:* including the development and management of marketing and proposals, services, resources, and supply chain.
- *Operations:* including customer relationship management, service management and operations, resource management and operations, and supplier/partner relationships management.
- *Enterprise Management:* including strategic and enterprise planning, enterprise risk management, enterprise effectiveness management, knowledge and research management, and financial and asset management. [8]

This model mirrors a functional model of a business and is thus not a business process model. It can however easily be converted to a Process model. This model decomposes into four levels of detail. Figure 9.2 shows the content of the eTOM model.

The distinguishing features of the eTOM model include that eTOM provides an industry-accepted Telecommunications Business Process Decomposition Model supporting:

- A process-oriented business model for use by service providers, vendors, and integrators.
- A common understanding of business processes and their linkages applicable across the industry.
- A basis for customizing and extending this common base to meet detailed, specific business needs.

Also included with eTOM is the definition and detail for:

- Process structure (hierarchy)
- Process decompositions (levels)
- Process flows (linkages)
- Process dynamics (behavior)

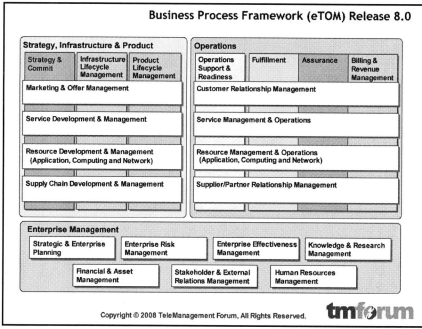

Figure 9.2

It is an industry-specific model that can be used for the Information and Communications Services Industry. This model includes processes such as customer relationship management (CRM) and supplier relationship management (SRM), processes not found in other models. This model contains processes for the developing and management of resources, processes not found in other models. This model contains detailed descriptions of the level four processes; this detail provides additional content to facilitate the development of a fifth level. None of the other models provide this content.

What are the gaps in the eTom model? This model does not contain processes for the financial and human resources functions.

Access to the eTOM Decomposition Model can be obtained by becoming a member of the TeleManagement Forum: tmforum.org.

APQC Process Classification Decomposition Model

APQC is the leading resource for performance analytics, best practices, process improvement, and knowledge management worldwide. Their research studies, benchmarking databases and renowned Knowledge Base provide managers with intelligence that they can use to transform their organizations for better results. A member-based nonprofit founded in 1977, APQC currently serves over 750 of the *Fortune* Global 1000 companies as well as hundreds of education and government organizations.

The Process Classification Framework^{SM} (PCF) was developed by APQC and member companies as an open standard to facilitate improvement through process management and benchmarking regardless of industry, size, or geography. The PCF organizes operating and management processes into 12 enterprise-level categories, including process groups and over 1,500 processes and associated activities. The PCF and associated measures and benchmarking surveys are available for download and completion at no cost at www.apqc.org.

Operating processes include: develop vision and strategy; design and develop products and services; market and sell products and services; deliver products and services; and manage customer service.

Management and support processes include: develop and manage human capital; manage information technology; manage financial resources; acquire, construct and manage property; manage environmental health and safety; manage external relationships; and manage knowledge, improvement, and change.

Regardless of size, industry, or geography, organizations can use the PCF to develop and optimize their business processes. [9]

The APQC Model is shown in Figure 9.3

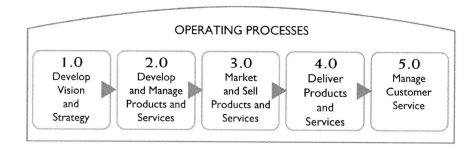

Figure 9.3

The distinguishing features of the AQPC model include:

- There are currently nine industry specific models available. The only other industry-specific model available is eTOM.
- It is the most complete model from a process coverage perspective since it covers most, if not all, processes in an organization.
- The model contains financial processes to some level of detail. Financial processes are either represented at a high level in other decomposition models, or not at all.

- The model contains IT processes that are also not present in other decomposition models. These IT processes can be further extended to support the Information Technology Infrastructure Library (ITIL) Service Support & Service Delivery processes. [13]
- It contains knowledge management processes that are also not present in other decomposition models.

What are the gaps in the AQPC model?
- Not all processes are developed to level four.
- The contents of the model do not always align from a level perspective.
- The twelve level one processes are not the same as business functions, but they could be seen as such. Any grouping of processes can lend itself to a silo view.
- Because the model is so robust there is sometimes an expectation that the model is complete. This is not so, e.g., the processes for managing employee benefits are missing from the financial processes.

Access to the APQC decomposition model can be obtained at apqc.org.

10. The Difference Between Business Processes and Business Functions

Business functions and business processes are often confused with each other. The development of business processes in the context of business functions (a/k/a, business silos) is arguably the single biggest reason business processes are sub optimized within an organization today. The confusing of business functions and business processes leads to two complications:

- Business processes are defined and described as functions.
- Business processes are developed within the context of functions.

Before we continue, let's provide a definition of a business function. A *business function* can be defined as a group or a department within a company that is responsible for fulfilling or executing activities in a process. Examples of business functions are finance, marketing, sales, and warehousing.

Business Processes are Defined and Described as Functions

Functions are often confused with processes, and also often co-exist with processes. This confusion sometimes arises because:

- Processes are grouped together, like grouping Manage and Retain Human Capital processes under a grouping called Human Resources (HR), which is a business function.
- Processes are described as business functions, e.g., HR.

The HR function is performed by an organization that is responsible for recruiting, managing benefits, and payroll. The payroll processes, however, cross multiple business functions such as HR and Finance.

Below is an example of a business process that has been described as a Functional Structure:

- 1.0 HR
    - o 1.1 Benefits
    - o 1.2 Payroll
    - o 1.3 Recruiting

The HR structure (1.0) is not a business process. There is no such thing as a process with the name HR. Neither is there a sub-process called Benefits. This structure is a grouping of business functions under the group HR.

The APQC Model (described in a later chapter) decomposes HR processes in the following way:

- 2.0 Develop and Manage Human Capital
    - o 2.1 Recruit, source and select employees
    - o 2.2 Reward and retain employees
        - • 2.2.1 Develop and manage reward recognition and motivation programs
        - • 2.2.2 Manage and administer benefits
        - • 2.2.3 Administrate payroll

Note how the APQC Model has Develop and Manage Human Capital as its main process, rather than HR. Here the focus is the *process* and the HR *functions* are not mentioned at all. There is a big difference between a *process* and which *function* is responsible for executing the process; we need to keep functions separate from processes.

Developing Processes Within the Context of Functions

Geary Rummler and Alan Brache coined the term "white space" in the late 1980's. The "white space" is the space between the departmental silos one finds on any organization chart. The white space consists of all the activities that reside in processes that cross from one business function to another.

Developing processes within functional boundaries means that all activities that fall within the white spaces are integration points – these are the integrations between processes and functions.

Let's review the processes that the payroll business function would perform.

- The human resources function administers payroll by performing payroll administration processes.
- Employee hours are captured via time keeping systems that are managed by the human resources function.
- Employee pay is typically calculated through the finance function by performing the manage employee pay processes.
- Payments are disbursed to bank accounts through the finance function by performing process and distribute payments processes.

If a business process project is confined to the accounting function, then the first two activities would be out of scope and ignored.

Scope has thus been defined by the business function and not the process itself.

Processes would thus not be developed from a total end-to-end perspective, but from a functional perspective. This would result in only part of the end-to-end process being developed. Sub-optimization is built into the processes, because when developed in this manner, process hand-offs and integration points with other processes, supported by other business functions, are not considered.

Payroll activities must include banking and financial activities. Money needs to be transferred to bank accounts so that employees can get paid. In which business functions do these processes belong? Do they reside within HR, the payroll, or the financial accounting function, or do they reside in a level one process called Finance?

The Solution to Process vs. Functions

To resolve the conflicts between processes and functions, an organization needs to:

- Approach business process optimization from an end-to-end perspective that covers all business functions, and not let business functions dictate scope.
- Develop end to end scenarios that that will combine multiple processes, and in doing so will cover multiple functions.

11. Define Requirements of the Business Process Ecosystem

An organization should do a thorough job of gathering requirements before commencing the development of the Business Process Ecosystem (BPE).

It is now time to identify who are the internal customers of this ecosystem and what are their requirements. Note that this activity will be more effective if the key stakeholders are educated first.

Customers of the Business Process Ecosystem will include:

- Process owners, or process stewards, who are employees that are charged to oversee the execution and continuous improvement of business processes.
- Employees who execute processes within the organization.
- The managers of the employees who execute the business processes.
- Resources allocated to Mergers and Acquisitions.
- Information Technology (IT) support personnel.

Remember, the internal customers mentioned here are the different groups or departments *within* the organization. Business partners (including customers) are represented in the business process decomposition and process flow diagrams, as well as business process support elements such as policies, procedures, and metrics.

Once internal customer requirements are gathered for the business process ecosystem, there is a need to further refine the requirements for the Business Process Decomposition Model. The requirements should trace back to some element of the Business Process Ecosystem.

Notes and Action Items

12. Define the Scope of the Ecosystem

The best way to define the scope of the ecosystem is to map customers (within your business) and their requirements to the components of the ecosystem. Figure 12.1 provides an example of possible requirements for the Business Process Ecosystem.

Group	Customer	Ecosystem Element
Business	Mergers and Acquisitions	Process Decomposition Model to level 3
	Human Resources	Role Definitions
I.T.	Security	Role Definitions and System Transactions

Figure 12.1

At this point it may be appropriate to identify new ecosystem elements. For example, the IT organization may want the ecosystem to consist of a Business Process Support Element for Web Services (SOA). Web Services could either be documented as a RICEF (Report, Interfaces, Conversions, Extensions and Forms) element, or as a new Business Process Support Element called Web Services.

The initial development of the ecosystem will occur through the execution of a project. Additions and maintenance of the ecosystem will provide further opportunities to extend the functionality and scope of the ecosystem.

Notes and Action Items

13. Define the Goals and Objectives for the Decomposition Model

Defining the goals and objectives for the process decomposition model is an important step, because these goals and objectives will directly impact how many levels deep the model should be. Key decisions to be made here are:

- *What should the content or scope of the decomposition model be?* Is the model to be developed for the whole organization, or is it going to be developed for a specific area of the business, or for a particular business unit, or for a particular process?

- *Are multiple models to be developed?* There may be a need to develop a different model for each business unit, if the organization consists of multiple and different business units. This is an option if the different businesses are not integrated.

- *How many levels deep does the Decomposition Model need to be?* Generic recommendations (without knowing your organization or requirements) are:
  - Develop four levels if the model is to be used for mergers and acquisitions only.
  - Develop five levels if not using the Decomposition Model to develop test plans explained earlier.
  - Develop six levels if you intend developing test plans from the Decomposition Model.

Notes and Action Items

14. Identify the Levels of the Decomposition Model

Define the term to be used for each level (i.e. process, process group, sub-process, activity, etc). This step will help communicate the content of the different levels.

Describing the levels will allow better understanding and communication of processes and to which level in the decomposition model a process belongs.

The important thing to remember here is that the current process nomenclature in the organization needs to be considered. If changes are made to the process vocabulary, a new language will be created and this will require extensive communication and change management.

Below are examples of the different process decomposition models and their level descriptions; these can be used to provide ideas for an organization's business process nomenclature. Each model and level is described by the level name first; an example of a process description for that level is described in parentheses.

The SCOR Model Has Three Levels
1. Process type (Plan, Source, Make)
2. Process category (Plan Make to Order, Plan Make to stock)
3. Process element (Identify Resources, Identify Requirements)

This is an example of a six level model developed for customers who wanted to use the SCOR Decomposition Model as the starting structure:
1. Process Chain (Supply Chain)
2. Process Type (Source)
3. Process Category (Source Make to order product)

4. Process Element (Identify Sourcing Requirements)
5. Task Group (Non-MRP Quotation)
6. Task (Forward RFQ to Procurement)

The eTOM decomposition model has four levels
1. Process Area (Operations)
2. Process Grouping (Customer Relationship Management)
3. Level 2 Processes (Support and Readiness)
4. Level 3 Processes (Support Customer Interface Management)

The APQC Decomposition Model has Four Levels
1. Category (Deliver products and services)
2. Process Groups (Plan and acquire resources)
3. Process (Manage demand for products and services)
4. Activity (Develop baseline forecasts)

15. Define Technology and Tools to Support the Ecosystem

As the contents of the business process ecosystem will effectively represent the process and knowledge capital of your organization, it should be supported by a technology solution.

Below are some questions to use as a guide in aiding the selection of a technology solution.

Access questions:
- Is there a need to make the ecosystem available to all or most employees?
- Is there a need to make the ecosystem available to management?
- Does the ecosystem need to be made available via the intranet/internet?
- Is remote access required?
- Does it need to have controlled access and be password secured?

Presentation questions:
- Does the ecosystem need to be made available via the intranet and Internet?

Integration questions:
- Do documents need to be attached to the Business Process Decomposition Model?
- Can the Business Process Support Elements be documents that are attachments, or do they need to be objects for reporting and analysis purposes, or both?

Content questions:
- Is there a need to represent end-to-end scenarios in the tool?

Notes and Action Items

Section Four: Developing the Business Process Ecosystem

This section covers the development of the Business Process Decomposition Model, and the end-to-end scenario views of the Business Process Decomposition Model.

The concept of process variants is introduced, including how to define them, and what to do with them once they are defined. How to represent them in the decomposition model is also covered in this section.

Chapter 16 describes preparation activities required before developing the business process decomposition model.

Chapter 17 describes the activities to develop the business process decomposition model from scratch.

Chapter 18 describes the activities to extend an existing process in a model.

Chapter 19 describes the activities to integrate content from both the APQC model and the SCOR model.

Chapter 20 covers potential applications for the decomposition model, as well as benefits of developing a process decomposition model.

Chapter 21 introduces readers to the concept of process variants and how to identify them.

Chapter 22 shows how process variants can be reflected in the process decomposition model.

Chapter 23 describes the concept of end-to-end processes, or scenario views.

Chapter 24 describes applications and benefits of developing a business process ecosystem.

The Business Process Ecosystem can now be developed. The steps needed include:

- Develop the Business Process Decomposition Model.
- Identify and develop business process variants.
- Develop process flow diagrams
- Develop End-to-End Scenario views of the Business Process Decomposition Model.
- Develop Business Process Support Elements.

16. Preparing to Develop the Business Process Decomposition Model

This chapter describes activities that should be completed in order to be fully prepared to begin development of the Business Process Decomposition Model. Model development can be done in three steps:

Step 1. Prepare and Educate the Team

- Assemble a small core team.
- Analyze the existing models available to you, and select the model that best fits your organization.
- Develop your rules for creating the decomposition model. (See sample rules below.)
- Define the scope of the model; are you developing a complete model, or starting with a particular process?
- Explain the concept of decomposition so that teams know what it is, and how to do it.

Step 2. Create, Validate, and Populate

- It is recommended to use the APQC model to help define the first level. If an organization is in the telecom industry you can either use the eTOM model as the starting point, or the APQC Telecom model.
- Develop the model initially with a small group and then later validate the decomposition model with a larger group. This exercise will be too time consuming and contentious if there is too large a group at the start.
- Start with one process and decompose it to the end number of levels that have been determined. Do this with a process that the group is familiar with and will feel comfortable in expanding. This process decomposition can be used as an example by other

teams who will be decomposing their own processes.

- Populate the model as much as possible, using the content from other models. Most organizations, irrespective of what industry they are in, can copy the IT, finance, and human resources processes from the APQC model and use these as a starting point.

Step 3. QA the Model

- A review needs to be made to see what the requirements for work instructions are, or what the lowest level of detail is.
- Define what is needed to be done with the lowest level. Consider within this discussion if there is a need to report on task and role combinations, task and transaction combinations, etc.
- Remember the scenario spreadsheet and raise the question: "Are some of the variables so different that another Level 2 or 3 process is needed?"
- Review your variants; the following chapter covers the identification and creation of variants. You will want to identify all your variants and ensure they are represented in the model.
- Ensure that items are non-redundant. In other words, don't repeat processes within or across branches of the "tree." If a process is repeated , it may need to be broken out into its own branch. This is a very important, yet a not-so-easy concept to recognize sometimes.

Things to Remember:

There is no need to start from scratch. Use as a starting point some of the existing models available to you. (If the industry you are developing for is not one of the delivered APQC industry models then refer to the information provided in Chapter 17.)

- If you are a manufacturing-centric organization, then you may want to use the APQC model as your baseline model, and then add SCOR model content to it (Deliver Products and Services). As a rule, I recommend adding the SCOR Enable process concept into any model that is developed.
- Copy the enabling process structure from the SCOR model. Its Level 3 processes will make your model more complete.
- Customers of SAP can also access their industry specific Solution

Maps to validate the model is complete.

- This is a not an organization chart. This is a process decomposition mode that does not have any reference to the organization structure.
- This is not a hierarchy of processes. No level within the model is more important than any another level.
- This is not a chart of functions in a business.
- When starting out don't try to be perfect: the review or validation cycles will help complete the model.
- Allow the team adequate time to brainstorm and develop the model.
- Continually check to ensure that items are non redundant (unless repeating for a variant).
- It is recommended to work in Excel, as Excel allows the documentation of a model that is wide.
- A critical lesson to remember is that it is very difficult to decompose one level at a time. If decomposed one level at a time the risk is run of adding activities that may not be correct for that level. In developing content for a particular level, consider the sub-processes in the next level of detail.

Rules for Decomposing

Before developing a model the team should review some rules for developing the model. The model development team can also develop their own set of rules. Below is a list of sample rules.

- Make the language specific to the organization. If the word "purchasing" is used in your organization instead of "procurement" or "source," then change the process descriptions accordingly.
- Ensure the name of the process adequately describes the proc esses.
- If there are more than eight processes, consider creating a new higher level process.
- Insist that each sub-process or activity starts with a verb. This helps ensure that processes represent actions to be performed (tasks to be performed) as opposed to department names (who is

performing the activities).

- Keep items at the "same level of detail" within a level of the hierarchy.
- Remember the lowest level of detail of a process is the level where:
  - The task cannot be broken down into smaller steps (i.e. print report).
  - It makes no sense to go into more detail.

17. Develop a New Model from Scratch

In this chapter we will cover developing a model from scratch. We will do this when the industry we are developing for is not one of the delivered APQC Industry models.

The industry we will use as an example is Higher Education.

Step 1. Create the Top-Level Tier

- Review the APQC model and identify which level one processes apply to your business, and which do not.
- Figure 17.1 is a first level of a model developed for a Business School.
- The following processes were retained:
  - Develop Vision and Strategy
  - All the Management & Support Processes
- Processes that were added are:
  - Develop & Publish Research
  - Design and Develop Courses
  - Market Institutional Offerings
  - Plan and Recruit Students
  - Deliver Educational Services

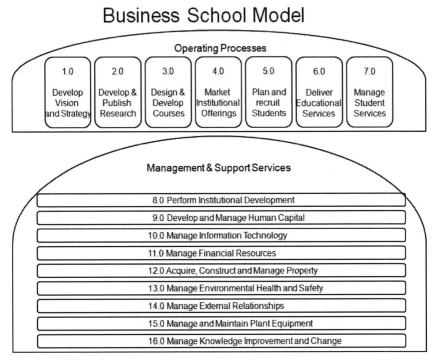

Figure 17.1

- From this first level can be seen:
    - o The operating processes are the core or strategic processes of the university.
    - o Processes 2.0 to 7.0 are all specific to a higher education organization.
    - o The Develop Vision and Strategy process is the same as per the APQC Model (parts of the APQC model have been leveraged).
    - o The Management & Support processes are the same as per the APQC model.

Step 2. Create Level 2

- Select the Level 1 process which you are now going to further decompose. In the case of our example we will select the Level 1 process, 2.0 Develop and Publish Research.
- Our development will follow a three step process:
    - Step 1 will be to identify the first step in the process. Here you need to consider how this process starts or get initiated.
    - Step 2 will be to identify the last step in the process. Here you need to consider how this process ends or what the terminating action is. (Our model now looks like figure 17.2.)

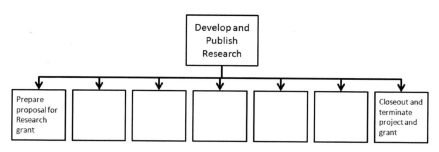

Figure 17.2

- Step 3 will be identifying the content between the first and last steps in the process.
    Here we will identify what processes we need to get from preparing a proposal to having the proposal completed and closed out. Some ideas are:
    - The proposal must be approved.
    - The research work must get done.
    - The work must be monitored. (Our model now looks like figure 17.3.)

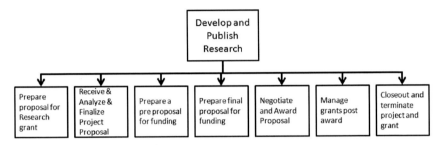

Figure 17.3

- The Level 2 processes for Develop and Publish Research are thus:
    - o Prepare proposal for Research grant
    - o Receive & Analyze & Finalize Project Proposal
    - o Prepare a pre proposal for funding
    - o Prepare final proposal for funding
    - o Negotiate and Award Proposal
    - o Manage grants post award
    - o Closeout and terminate project and grant

Step 3. Create Level 3
- Once again select the Level 2 process which you are now going to further decompose. In the case of our example we will select the Level 2 process, Prepare final proposal for funding.
- Our development will follow a three step process:
    - o Step 1 will be to identify the first step in the process. Here you need to consider how this process starts or get initiated.
    - o Step 2 will be to identify the last step in the process. Here you need to consider how this process ends or what the terminating action is. (Our model now looks like figure 17.4.)

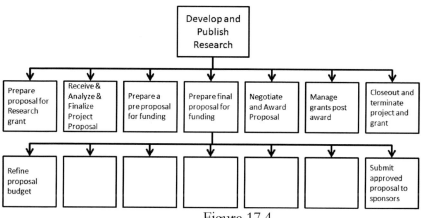

Figure 17.4

○ Step 3 will be identify the content between the first and last steps in the process.
Here we will identify what processes we need to get from preparing a proposal to having the proposal completed and closed out. Some ideas are:

- The proposal must be approved.
- The research work must get done.
- The work must be monitored. (Our model now looks like figure 17.5.)

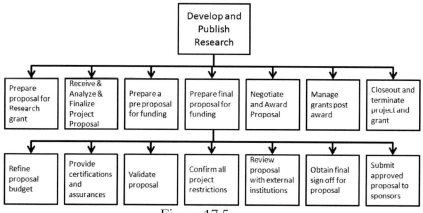

Figure 17.5

- The Level 3 processes for Prepare final proposal for funding are thus:
  - Refine proposal budget
  - Provide certifications and assurances
  - Validate proposal
  - Confirm all project restrictions
  - Review proposal with external institutions
  - Obtain final sign off for proposal
  - Submit approved proposal to sponsors

Step 4. Create Level 4 to N levels
- Follow the above processes to develop all further levels.
- If your model is six levels deep, ensure that this is the lowest level of detail. Add your systems transactions and manual activities at level six.

18. Extend an Existing Process in the Model

In this chapter we will extend an existing process in the APQC model to Level 5, and then to 6. In the model below we see that Process journal entries is a Level 4 process, with the number 8.3.2.2. We will extend this process.

8.3   Perform general accounting and reporting
    8.3.1   Manage policies and procedures
        8.3.1.1   Negotiate service level agreements
        8.3.1.2   Establish accounting policies
        8.3.1.3   Set and enforce approval limits
        8.3.1.4   Establish common financial systems
    8.3.2   Perform general accounting
        8.3.2.1   Maintain chart of accounts
        8.3.2.2   Process journal entries
        8.3.2.3   Process allocations
        8.3.2.4   Process period end adjustments (e.g., accruals, currency conversions, etc.)
        8.3.2.5   Post and reconcile intercompany transactions
        8.3.2.6   Reconcile GL accounts
        8.3.2.7   Perform consolidations and process eliminations
        8.3.2.8   Prepare trial balance
        8.3.2.9   Prepare and post management adjustments

Step 1. Create Level 5

- Our development will follow a three step process:
  - o Step 1 will be to identify the first step in the process. Here you need to consider how this process starts or get initiated.
  - o Step 2 will be to identify the last step in the process. Here you need to consider how this process ends or what the terminating action is. (Our model now looks like figure 18.1.)

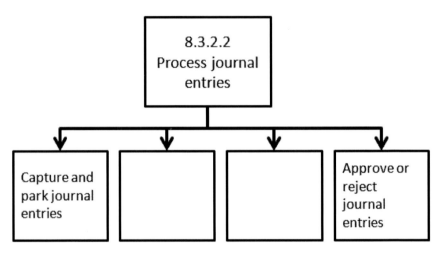

Figure 18.1

  - o Step 3 will be identifying the content between the first and last steps in the process.

    Here we will identify what processes we need to get from capturing a journal entry to obtain approval. Some ideas are:
    - Routing journal entries to authorized approvers
    - Deleting journal entries (Our model now looks like figure 18.2.)

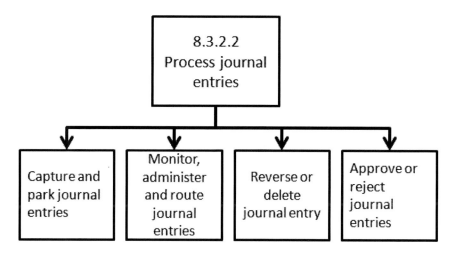

Figure 18.2

Step 2. Create Level 6

Remember, Level 6 is our lowest level of detail, so it should consist of manual activities and systems related activities.

- Our development will follow a three step process:
    - o Step 1 will be to identify the first step in the process. Here you need to consider how this process starts or get initiated.
    - o Step 2 will be to identify the last step in the process. Here you need to consider how this process ends or what the terminating action is. (Our model now looks like figure 18.3.)

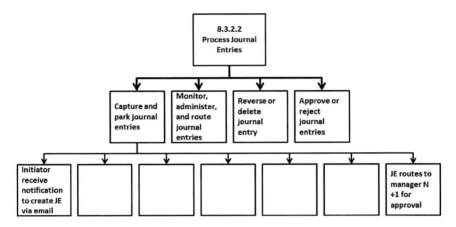

Figure 18.3

   o   Step 3 will be identifying the content between the first and last steps in the process.
Here we will identify what processes we need to get from capturing a journal entry to obtaining approval. Some ideas are:

- Routing journal entries to authorized approvers
- Deleting journal entries (Our model now looks like figure 18.4)

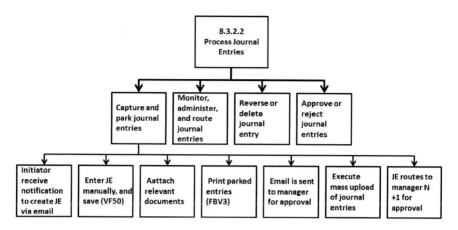

Figure 18.4

Notes and Action Items

19. Integrate APQC and SCOR Model Content

In this chapter we will integrate the SCOR model; and Enable Process content into the APQC model. Let's first discuss why you would want to merge SCOR content with the APQC model.

The APQC model is incomplete in some process areas, and you will want to add more content, which could be readily available in the SCOR model.

The SCOR Enable process concept groups all support processes (not core to the process), and this allows you to add this content to your model.

The SCOR model has the supply chain content already developed, so there is no need for you to reinvent it. The SCOR model Enable Source processes are listed below:

ES1. Manage Sourcing Business Rules

ES2. Assess Supplier performance

ES3. Maintain source data

ES4. Manage product inventory

ES5. Manage capital assets

ES6 Manage incoming product

ES7. Manage Supplier network

ES8. Manage Import/Export requirements

ES9. Manage supplier agreements

A review of the APQC model shows the following procurement or source processes:

4.2   Procure materials and services

   4.2.1   Develop sourcing strategies

      4.2.1.1   Develop procurement plan

      4.2.1.2   Clarify purchasing requirements

      4.2.1.3   Develop inventory strategy

4.2.1.4   Match needs to supply capabilities
4.2.1.5   Analyze company's spend profile
4.2.1.6   Seek opportunities to improve efficiency and value
4.2.1.7   Collaborate with suppliers to identify sourcing
            opportunities
  4.2.2   Select suppliers and develop/maintain contracts
4.2.2.1   Select suppliers
4.2.2.2   Certify and validate suppliers
4.2.2.3   Negotiate contracts
4.2.2.4   Manage contracts
  4.2.3   Order materials and services
4.2.3.1   Process/Review requisitions
4.2.3.2   Approve requisitions
4.2.3.3   Solicit/Track vendor quotes
4.2.3.4   Create/Distribute purchase orders
4.2.3.5   Expedite orders and satisfy inquiries
4.2.3.6   Record receipt of goods
4.2.3.7   Research/Resolve exceptions
  4.2.4   Appraise and develop suppliers
4.2.4.1   Monitor/Manage supplier information
4.2.4.2   Prepare/Analyze procurement and vendor
            performance
4.2.4.3   Support inventory and production processes
4.2.4.4   Monitor quality of product delivered
  4.2.5   Implement procurement initiatives
4.2.5.1   Implement cross-functional buying teams
4.2.5.2   Implement buying consortiums
4.2.5.3   Implement integrated supply
4.2.5.4   Implement e-procurement
4.2.5.5   Implement purchasing cost reduction program

A mapping of the two models shows the following:
ES1. Manage Sourcing Business Rules – not in APQC model
ES2. Assess Supplier performance – same as APQC model
        4.2.4.2 Prepare/Analyze procurement and vendor performance.
ES3. Maintain source data – not found in APQC model

ES4. Manage product inventory – same as APQC model
   4.5.3.7 Manage physical finished goods inventory
ES5. Manage capital assets – same as APQC model
   8.3.3.9 Track fixed assets including physical inventory
ES6 Manage incoming product – same as APQC model
   4.5.2.2   Manage inbound material flow
ES7. Manage Supplier network – not found in APQC model
ES8. Manage Import/Export requirements – not in APQC model
ES9. Manage supplier agreements– same as APQC model
   4.2.2   Select suppliers and develop/maintain contracts

To integrate the two models do the following:
- Add a new process named Manage and Support Procurement at Level 3 as (4.3.1).
- Add the following processes as Level 4 processes:
   4.3.1.1 Manage sourcing business rules
   4.3.1.2 Maintain source data
   4.3.1.3 Manage supplier network
   4.3.1.4 Manage import/export requirements

Notes and Action Items

20. Business Process Decomposition Model: Applications and Benefits

Applications for the Business Process Decomposition Model

A Business Process Decomposition Model is a flexible tool that has numerous applications, and that can be used many times over for a variety of business process activities. Below are some applications of the Business Process Decomposition Model:

Provides the Ability to Analyze an Organization's Existing Processes and to Develop New Processes

The macro view provided by the process decomposition model facilitates the easy analysis of processes as well as the identification of integration points between processes because multiple processes can be viewed at the same time.

Can be Used to Perform Fit Gap Analysis Against Software and ERP Systems

This tool improves the quality of business process definition efforts and gap analysis by allowing gap analysis to be done from a Business Process perspective as gaps can be identified and documented at Level 3 or Level 4 of the model.

Can be Used for Mergers and Acquisitions

Facilitates a rapid assessment of an organization's processes, and the subsequent gap analysis can be structured in such a way that an organization's strengths and weaknesses can easily be identified by mapping the new organization to the decomposition model.

Can be Used for Requirements Gathering

Requirements can easily be gathered at any level of the business process decomposition model by gathering requirements from a business process perspective and documenting them at Level 3 or

Level 4 of the model.

Can be Used to Develop Test Plans for ERP/Software Projects

Unit test plans can be developed using Level 3 or Level 4 of the Process Decomposition Model. Unit tests are defined as testing within a process; an example of a unit test is testing the creation of a purchase order and a goods receipt.

Integration test plans can be developed from the end-to-end scenarios created as alternate views of the Process Decomposition Model. Integration tests are defined as tests that cross processes. An example of an integration test is a test that consists of planning, procurement, receiving, and inbound logistics processes.

Benefits of Developing the Business Process Decomposition Model

The Business Process Decomposition Model is the Foundation of the Business Process Ecosystem

- It is the best tool for identifying and providing a snapshot of all the business processes within an organization.
- It is the best tool to identify integration points between different processes as the decomposition model provides visibility of multiple processes.
- It provides the best structure to develop and define end-to-end business scenarios.
- It provides the best structure to identify, develop, and associate the business process support elements.

Facilitates the Identification of all Business Processes

The structure of the Business Process Decomposition Model facilitates the identification of all business processes and reduces or eliminates the surprises of identifying missed processes later on in a project.

Provides an Organization with a Common Frame of Reference for its Business Processes

A Business Process Decomposition Model defines terms and creates a perspective for personnel to see what the models are, what processes they address, and how they work. This provides an organization a common frame of reference and a common terminology to see how all processes are integrated.

Provides Structure to Business Process Definition Initiatives

- It has traditionally been difficult to estimate the number of resources required and the effort required for business process projects. These efforts would be easier to estimate if a decomposition model were developed first. Average development duration efforts can be applied to each process, and the Level 3 or 4 processes can be tabulated, and the work effort could be calculated. The decomposition model can be used to scope, size, and staff process initiatives.
- It is a structure that facilitates scope management and project management of all process initiatives.
- It is a structure that facilitates the identification of cross-functional activities and handoffs required to achieve the business or process goals.
- It is a structure that identifies all the processes in a business.

Therefore, an embedded structure will enable the estimating of the time it takes to complete or do process mapping, or estimate the number of resources that are required by counting the number of processes there are at Levels 3 and 4. Based on these counts, the number of resources required for a project can be estimated.

The result of providing the structure beforehand eliminates the confusion as to what should be in a flow diagram. One of the greatest time wasters in any business process initiative is the debating over what the content of a process flow diagram should be. The business process decomposition model content should be the content of the process flow diagrams.

Most process initiatives are started in the middle. That is, some companies identify a critical process and decide to redesign it without regard to other processes. The redesign effort also starts with drawing process flow diagrams. The problems with this approach are:

- The scope and boundaries of the process are very difficult to define without considering other processes.

- Process initiatives also typically start with core processes and not much thought is given to the support or enabling processes, which are often as complex as the core processes they support.
- It is very difficult to understand where these processes fit into the overall schema of what the business does.

Reduces Time it Takes to Develop Business Process Flow Diagrams

The Business Process Decomposition Model defines the content of Process Flow Diagrams and thus reduces the time it takes to develop them; because the diagram content is already established.

Provides Structure to Business Process Optimization and Improvement Initiatives

The macro view that the Process Decomposition Model provides, makes it easy to identify integration points between processes, since multiple processes can be viewed at the same time.

The Process Decomposition Model allows process optimization teams to see how processes relate to each other. It is very difficult to see this if only process flow diagrams are developed.

21. Identify Process Variants

A process variant is a variation of a standard business process. It is necessary to identify your process variants, because you need to add them into the process model.

The best way to explain process variants is with an example.

Most, if not all organizations buy goods and services. These organizations will therefore have a procurement process with some or all of the steps below:

- An employee creates or fills out a requisition to buy something.
- The requisition follows an approval process and gets approved or rejected.
- Once approved, a purchase order is created and sent to the supplier.
- The purchased product is delivered by the supplier and received at the buying organization.
- Accounts payable is notified to pay the supplier.

There are multiple variations of the above process:

- Items to be bought can range from stationery to raw materials for manufacturing, utilities such as energy and water, and services such as window cleaning. These items are thus variants.
- Each of the items listed above may require a different approval process (or none at all).
- Some purchased items may require an extra process step, such as a quality control check for the raw materials purchased for manufacturing.
- There is no formal receiving step for receiving services or non-physical items.
- The suppliers can be either local or located overseas, which may require different processes or additional process steps.

Each of the variations above may result in additional process steps and may require different data to enable execution. There are two types of variations or variants of a business process.

1. *Process Variant:* depending on the product, customer or site, the process steps or activities are different.

2. *Data Variant:* depending on the product, customer or site, the process steps or activities are NOT different, but the data needed for the process variant is different. For example, if customers are segmented by customer type (for reporting purposes), customer type would be a data variant.

In developing the BPDM we will consider the process variants only. The data variants should not be added to the model, as these will be covered by the systems transaction BPSE, or at the work instruction level.

The main reasons for developing process variants are:

- Identifying variants will assist in the complete definition of all business processes

- This is the best way to *identify* all the variations and nuances of business processes.

- One of the main reasons ERP implementation projects are delayed is the process variants are not identified and developed; doing this step will avoid this.

- This is the starting point for developing the integration test plan. A project can use these scenario variants to develop integration test plans.

Steps for developing process variants:

Develop a spreadsheet for each of the key processes or scenarios (i.e., Lead to Cash, Procure to Pay, etc). Consider doing this for relevant support processes as well. Use Level 3 or level content from your decomposition model.

Figure 21.1 shows variants for a sales order process. Note that this is by no means complete, as there would typically have to be columns for contract types, payment terms, customer attributes, as well as many other items. Add a column for every item that could have a variation. Note that this example does not distinguish between data or process variants.

Customer Type	Sales Channel	Sales Division	Sales Offering	Delivery Source
SMB	OEM	ABC	Installation services	USA ware-house
Govt, GSA	Direct out-side	Europe West	Configurable items	Europe warehouse
OEM	Direct in-side	Europe East	Stock items - hardware	Partner (drop ship)
National Acct	Website	USA Div1	Stock items - software	SA ware-house
Strategic Acct	Manuf. reps	USA Div2	Training services	HQ

Figure 21.1

Column 1 shows the types of customers that buy from this business.
Column 2 lists the different sales channels that sell the product.
Column 3 lists the different sales divisions that either own the product, sell the product, or will get sales revenue credit for the sale.
Column 4 lists all the products and services a customer would buy.
Column 5 lists from where goods or products are delivered.

From the example, note there are the following *data* variants:
Delivery sources: There will be a different code for each delivery location.
Sales channels: There will be a different code for each channel.
Customer groups: There will be a different code for each type of customer.

From the example, note there are the following *process* variants:

Delivery sources: different process steps or activities depending on whether the product is delivered from South America or Europe versus a local warehouse.

Delivery logistics: The delivery variants will follow different logistic processes; for example, the drop ship process is different from the shipping process that is expedited with FedEx.

Benefits of developing process variants include:

- This is the most complete method to identify all the variations in the processes. This means there will be no chance of forgetting to identify any processes and there will be no surprises later in the project.
- This assists in developing the integration test plan. It jump-starts the development of test plans.
- This provides guidance on what processes to test.
- This facilitates business rules discussions that focus on how variations will be handled.
- This is an effective method for identifying how often a scenario variant occurs.
- This facilitates the assigning of priorities to all variants.

22. Identify How Variants will be Reflected in the Model

This is the act of identifying and analyzing business process variants and deciding how they will be represented in the process decomposition model and at what level in the model. Process variants must be represented in the decomposition model to ensure its completeness. The SCOR model deals with process variants in the following ways:

- The Level 1 SCOR model processes are Plan, Source, Make, Deliver and Return.
- The Level 2 SCOR model processes for Source are:
    o Source Make to Order (MTO)
    o Source Make to Stock (MTS)
    o Source Engineer to Order (ETO)
- The Level 3 SCOR model processes for Source Make to Order are:
    o Schedule Product Deliveries
    o Receive Product
    o Verify Product
    o Transfer Product
    o Authorize Supplier Payment
- The Level 3 SCOR model processes for Source Make to Stock are:
    o Schedule Product Deliveries
    o Receive Product
    o Verify Product
    o Transfer Product
    o Authorize Supplier Payment

- The Level 3 SCOR model processes for Source Engineer to Order are:
    - Schedule Product Deliveries
    - Receive Product
    - Verify Product
    - Transfer Product
    - Authorize Supplier Payment

As shown in the above processes, variants are represented in the model at Level 2. There is some repetition of processes at Level 3 (Receive Product, Verify Product).

There are two schools of thought on how to deal with process variants:

(1) Deal with variants as per the SCOR Model, at a high level in the Process Decomposition Model.

(2) Deal with variants at a level lower (at Level 5 or 6 in the decomposition model). Here the process variant is defined at the point it occurs in the process. The benefit of defining variants at this lower level is that it reduces the number of processes that are replicated in the model.

The choice on how to deal with these variants in the model is dependent on a few factors:

- How variable is the process variant? If the sub-processes of the variants are mostly the same, then define the variants at Level 5 or Level 6 in the decomposition model.
- What type of variant is it? For example, a company that manufactures different types of products may want to define process variants by product type (i.e., processes for dealing with configurable products will be different from make to stock or make to plan products). In this case, variants should be shown at a higher level in the model.

Note that there is no need to show all the variants in the decomposition model, it is only necessary to show the process variants and not the data variants in the model.

23. Develop End-to-End Scenario Views

This chapter covers the development of the end-to-end scenario views of the Business Process Decomposition Model.

It also covers the concept of process variants, and how to define them, and what to do with them once they are defined.

How to Represent Scenario Views in the Business Process Decomposition Model

This is the creation of multiple and different views of the Business Process Decomposition Model (BPDM) for the purposes of creating end-to-end processes or scenarios. Scenario views are meta processes that cross multiple Level 1 or Level 2 processes of the Decomposition Model. An organization would develop scenarios if it has process owners and has defined their scope as being a grouping of processes, such as the Student Value Chain. The values of end-to-end scenario views of the BPDM include:

- Provide process owners and supply chain managers a view of all their processes.
- Facilitate the development of scenario measurements or metrics.
- Identify which Level 2 or Level 3 processes make up this scenario.
- Document the new scenario by attaching the processes previously identified.

Scenario views of the BPDM:

- Provide a scenario view of the Business Process Decomposition Model.
- Enable more usage and participation in the Decomposition Model as the model has multiple and different uses depending on the audience (integration analysts, supply chain analysts, etc.).

- Provide end-to-end views of business processes. This allows business process optimization efforts to consider an end-to-end process.
- Scenario views of the BPDM can be used to generate test plans.

Benefits of Developing Scenario Views

Process Optimization

- Process optimization efforts needs to consider complete end-to-end processes. The biggest improvement opportunities exist in the white space (which is described as the integration points between different business processes). Combining multiple end-to-end processes will facilitate process optimization activities.

Systems and Software Implementations

- Computer systems and ERP systems need to be set up or configured to enable the business processes of an organization. These systems need to be set up in an integrated manner.
- The best way to test that these integrated processes have been set up correctly, is to test them as integrated processes. Test Plans must include testing of stand-alone processes such as the Returns Process, or the integrated process that includes Planning, Procure to Pay, and the Manage Inbound Logistics processes.

Process Access and Usage

- Developing end-to-end scenarios will allow processes to be viewed in their entirety and not only within their functional silos.
- Scenario views will provide internal customers a different viewpoint and entry point to the process decomposition model.
- Scenario views provide alternate views of the Business Process Decomposition Model.
- Scenario views enable expanded uses of the model as the model will have different uses depending on the audience: integration analysts, supply chain analysts, etc.

24. Applications and Benefits of Developing the Business Process Ecosystem

This chapter describes applications and benefits of the business process ecosystem.

Organization Mindset

The Business Process Ecosystem will assist in moving an organization to a process mindset:

- Processes will be described as processes instead of functions.
- Processes will be identified in the model.
- Business Process Support Elements will be developed to improve the execution of business processes.
- Metrics and Reporting will provide the organization the information needed to manage and optimize the business processes.

Business Process Development

- The Business Process Ecosystem provides the ability to fully scope a business process project. All business processes and process support elements can be identified.
- Developing a decomposition model will enable the identification of all business processes and then support elements can be classified.
- The Business Process Ecosystem will allow for the identification of all work and deliverables to be developed. This will provide a view to management or project sponsors of what *done* looks like, with a clear definition of deliverables.
- The Business Process Ecosystem provides tools to enable employees to execute processes flawlessly (access to all process ecosystem documentation).

- Process execution will be improved as all users will have the required policies, business rules, procedures, and work instructions available to them. This will reduce or prevent processing errors.

Business Process Support and Maintenance

- The Business Process Ecosystem provides support personnel tools to enable the support of business and IT solutions.

Business Process Optimization Initiatives

- The Business Process Decomposition Model is a tool that facilitates business process optimization as it can be used to identify business process improvement opportunities as it provides the ability to show dependencies and integration points between multiple processes.
- Business Process Optimization initiatives can also be improved if a sound process baseline is established. This baseline is the decomposition model.

Communication

- Business communication is improved as the business processes and their support documentation can be made available to the organization.

Improved Quality of Business Process Initiatives

- The process framework is a complete view of an organizations processes as it starts with a macro view of all processes, consists of process flow diagrams at a more detailed view, and culminates with the highest level of detail in the form of work instructions, which explain in detail how to perform tasks.
- The three-tier business process framework facilitates the identification of all business processes.
- The business process decomposition model provides the context and structure for a business process definition effort. Developing a business process decomposition model should be the first step in any business process definition effort.

- The Business Process Decomposition Model facilitates the identification of all the business processes within an organization. Processes are thus not "forgotten" or missed during process definition.

Faster Delivery and Completion of Business Process Projects

- Projects can be scoped quicker with the use of the decomposition model.
- Development of Process Flow Diagrams will be quicker as there will be little or no debate as to their content, as the content of the process flow diagrams will have a consistent level of detail.

Improved Organization Change Management

- Workers or end users will be catered to. They will know that the work instructions will be developed to guide them through work activities.
- The development of work instructions is typically ignored or only thought of at the end of business process initiatives. Sometimes they are identified only during training when someone asks, "How does my job change," or "What is my new job?" This is the level where work gets done by workers, so in reality this should be the most important step in any business process definition exercise.

Improved Operations

- Having detailed work instructions will allow employees to understand their jobs better and thus be more efficient and this will eliminate errors and rework.

Notes and Action Items

Section Five: Developing Business Process Support Elements

For a business process to be properly developed, executed, measured, managed, and optimized, it needs much more than a process flow diagram. A business process needs a number of supporting constructs. It is important to understand the types and nature of these support elements, because as processes are developed or changed, so should these process support elements be changed.

Business process support elements can best be described as the supporting constructs that allow a business process to be developed, executed, measured, managed, and optimized.

This section explains the different business process support elements and provides guidance to developing them.

Below are some examples of business process support elements that a business process requires:

- Business process activities are performed by people, thus an element of a business process is the role definition for that person.

- Security controls and the profiles of resources and the systems and the transactions they can access are another process support element.

- A business process activity is governed by rules that bound the execution of the activity. These rules are sometimes documented in policies. Rules are a type of process support element.

- A business process often has activities that are supported or enabled by an IT system or ERP system. An element of a process is thus the IT system or ERP system transaction and, more specifically, instructions on how to execute the transaction.

- A business process is often supported by a computer system. The data the computer system requires is a process support element.

- With the high profile of Sarbanes-Oxley law and other compliance regulations, another element of a process has become more important and noticeable. These are the controls or compliance controls for the business processes.

- Process measurements and metrics can also be elements of a process. It can be argued that not all processes have or need metrics, but it still makes sense to add this element for those processes that do have metrics.

- Reports, Interfaces, Conversions, Enhancements and Forms (RICEF) objects. A process is also supported by RICEF objects. These objects need to be identified, defined, developed, documented, communicated, and made accessible to those executing or supporting the processes.

- Knowledge Management or Organizational Learning. Processes that involve problem resolution often have as a base or input a historical view of previous problems encountered and their solutions. The capture and use of organization learning or organization knowledge can also be seen as process support elements.

Chapter 25 explains the development of process flow diagrams.

Chapter 26 explains role definitions and the importance of creating them.

Chapter 27 reviews systems security controls and how they are used to allow or prevent systems accesses.

Chapter 28 introduces business rules.

Chapter 29 covers policies.

Chapter 30 covers procedures.

Chapter 31 shows how processes, business rules, policies and procedures are integrated and support each other.

Chapter 32 explains work instructions.

Chapter 33 covers systems transactions.

Chapter 34 introduces data standards and how they support system transactions.

Chapter 35 reviews process controls.

Chapter 36 covers metrics and Key Performance Indicators (KPIs) and explains the difference between them.

Chapter 37 explains the concept of RICEF elements and how they support business processes.

Chapter 38 explains knowledge management, and how it can enable a process to be more effective.

Chapter 40 provides some direction towards developing a business process ecosystem.

Notes and Action Items

25. Process Flow Diagrams

A Process Flow Diagram (PFD) is the graphical representation of the steps or activities of a business process. The development of process flow diagrams can be simplified and accelerated if a process decomposition model is developed first. Figure 25.1 is a representation of this portion of a decomposition model.

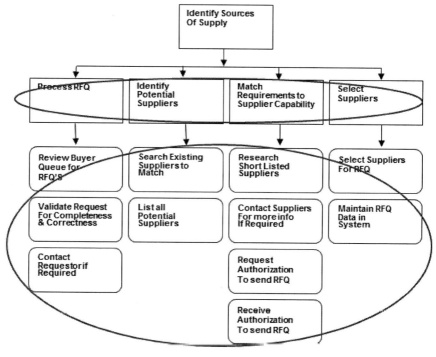

Figure 25.1

The following is an approach to developing process flow diagrams:

- We will develop the process flow diagrams by following the structure of the decomposition model.
- There are two options for developing a process flow for the process "Identify sources of supply."

- Option 1, is to develop the flow diagram containing the Level 4 processes only. Figure 25.2 shows the four Level 4 processes, there are no other processes shown in this diagram.

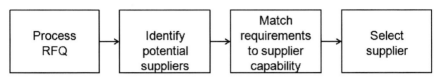

Figure 25.2

- Option 2 is to develop the flow diagram containing the Level 5 processes only. Figure 25.3 shows the eleven Level 5 processes. The Level 5 processes: Process RFQ, Identify suppliers, Match requirements, and Select suppliers must not be reflected in the process diagram. Note that with option 2, the Level 4 processes are not shown.

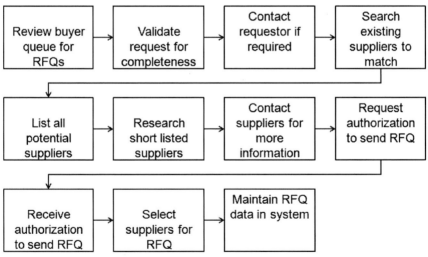

Figure 25.3

Developing Flow Diagrams with Swim Lanes

Figure 25.4 shows a process flow diagram with swim lanes. Swim lanes are horizontal lanes in a flow diagram that show which organization or business function is performing any particular activity. In our example the three functions that process requisitions are the requestor, the requestor's manager, and the purchasing organization who either converts requisitions to purchase orders or closes out any rejected requisitions.

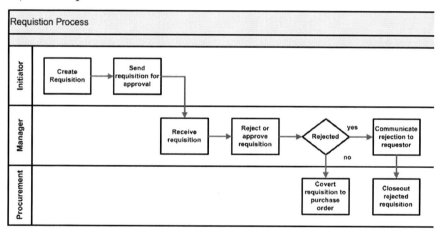

Figure 25.4

Do's and don'ts:

- Do develop the decomposition model first before developing process flow diagrams.
- Do define standards and naming conventions for content in the process flow diagrams.
- Do define standards for shapes in the flows.
- Don't mix and match levels in the process flow diagram. Avoid this by following the rules above.
- The content of the process flow diagrams must be the content of the decomposition model.

Remember, the levels of the decomposition model clearly helps identify what the content of a process flow diagram should be. If this method of developing Process Flow Diagrams is followed, the level of the content in the process flow diagrams will be consistent.

Advantages for developing process flow diagrams are:
- Process flow diagrams facilitate the understanding of how a process is executed.
- Process flow diagrams are a good visual representation of a process and have proved to be the best way to document a process.
- It is easier to follow and understand a business process if it is represented in a graphical format. This graphical format facilitates the communication of how a process is executed.
- It is easier to follow a graphical representation of decision points and process loops in a business process flow diagram as opposed to a text description.
- Flow diagrams provide all employees in an organization with a common process language.

Listed below are benefits to developing process flow diagrams:
- Process flow diagrams facilitate the communication of a business process, and allows for better understanding of a process.
- Process flow diagrams reveal opportunities for improvement.
- Process activities are assigned to organization units or roles in horizontal swim lanes. This is the first time an organizational element is applied to the business process ecosystem.

26. Role Definitions

A role is a named collection of users and permissions. A role definition is a named collection of tasks that specify which tasks a user or groups of users are allowed to perform. A role definition describes the activities for each individual role. A role is not a job, but rather a job is made up of a number of roles. An employee can thus have one or many roles assigned to them. Role definitions should be developed for the following reasons:

- Role definitions are an important tool that is used to guide employees in performing process activities and to explain their role in the performance of a business process.
- Role definition for systems security management is an important aspect of internal control and risk management.
- A role allows the grouping of permissions (i.e. a goods receiver needs to access a series of system transactions).
- Roles can be a convenience when developing and communicating organization policy.

Steps to develop job descriptions

- Identify the types of roles you need. This can be done by either reviewing existing roles, or by reviewing your process model and identifying the roles required. Another approach is to identify roles by job function. List all the job functions in the organization and create roles for these job functions. If a person does goods receiving, then there should be a goods receiving job role.
- Setup a team to define the roles. The manager to whom the position will report takes the lead to develop a job description, but other employees who are performing similar jobs can contribute as well.
- Research similar roles for ideas around tasks, responsibilities, etc. Perform a job analysis.
- Develop the role description. Role definition templates, docu-

ments, or systems should contain some or all of these elements:

- o Role summary
- o Roles descriptions
- o Role responsibilities
- o Success requirements in key result areas
- o Education requirements
- o Skills requirements
- o Training requirements
- o Security profiles
- o System transaction profiles

Review the role description, and obtain final approvals from human resources. As an example, and while varying from organization to organization, the procurement process requires, at a minimum, that the following roles be supported:

- Purchase item requestor (or requisition creator)
- Purchase item authorizer
- Purchase order creator
- Goods receiver
- Accounts payer

The benefits of developing role definitions

- Role definitions explain job activities and set clear expectations. This makes it very clear for employees what is expected of them.
- They allow their management to manage and track performance of employees against defined responsibilities.
- They assist in the definition of recruiting requirements.

27. System Security Controls

Security controls are the access permissions that are set up for a system that allows and restricts users to different system transactions. Security controls can be defined as the controls implemented to limit access and authority for system transactions and/or data. Security access levels are typically assigned to roles and not individual employees. The definition of roles and the subsequent assigning of employees to roles is thus a precursor to defining security controls. The reasons for developing security controls are:

- It is necessary to develop security controls as most computer systems require controlled access to the system transactions.
- It facilitates the easier maintenance of system access privileges by role rather than by allocating individual transactions to users.
- It enforces the Sarbanes-Oxley Act requirement for the segregation of duties.

Steps to develop Security Controls

- Figure 27.1 is an example of a table or spreadsheet developed by listing roles and their high level descriptions, and then listing all the system transactions that the role needs to perform the job function.
- The table is typically developed for a SAP Project. System Transaction codes are assigned to roles and profiles. System security personnel use these tables to assist in setting up user profiles into a security system.
- Once this table or spreadsheet is developed, it can be passed onto security administration personnel who will administer the role system access privileges.

Role	Profile	Description	TCode	Description
Buyer	ZPR Buyers	Buyer in purchasing division	FB03	Display Document
			FB04	Document changes
			FBL1	Display vendor line items
			FBL3	Display GL account line items
			FK03	Display vendor

Figure 27.1

Benefits of developing security controls include:
- Provides for the easier definition of system accesses because of role-based security permissions.
- Facilitates controlled access of system transactions and reports.
- Shows segregation of duties during compliance audits.

28. Business Rules

A business rule is a statement that defines or constrains some aspect of the business. It is intended to assert business structure or to control and influence the behavior of customers and employees of the business. For example, a business rule might state that *no product returns will be accepted without a receipt.* In this example, customer behaviors are influenced by the requirement to supply the purchase receipt when they return any product. The behaviors of employees who work in receiving are also influenced, as they will need to validate that the purchase receipt is valid for the returned item.

Business rules are not descriptions of a process or processing, but definitions of the conditions under which a process is carried out or the new conditions that will exist after a process has been completed. (The word *process* is used here in the general sense.)

Business rules should not be confused with workflow rules. They are different, and they should be identified separately from each other. Business rules govern an organization, regardless of the process or procedure chosen to execute them. Workflow rules, by contrast, define *how* work is done. Workflow rules define the process by which business is done; they are bound by the business rules.

Characteristics of business rules

- A business rule is a statement of truth or fact about an organization. It is an attempt to *describe* the operations of an organization.
- A rule is either completely true or completely false. The rule for returns states: *"no product returns will be accepted without a receipt."* This is an emphatic statement: *no receipt means no returns.*
- Business rules are distinct, independent constructs from business processes.
- Business rules are expressed in business language, and not in technical terms. Business rules are business and not technology oriented. For example, a company's business rules should be understandable to a knowledgeable customer.

- Business rules are developed and owned by the business. They can, however, be implemented by technology or implementation teams.

Steps for developing business rules

The Process Scenario Variant spreadsheet and the decomposition model are guides that will assist in identifying where business rules are needed.

Review the decomposition model (Levels 3 to 6) and identify all processes and sub processes that require business rules. The process of identifying rules is an iterative process, this exercise will therefore be repeated many times.

Consider these questions for each process and sub-process:
- Is the process clearly understood? Does it need more explaining?
- Is a rule needed?
- Under what conditions should the process be executed?
- Under what conditions should the process not be executed?

Each rule developed should have the following characteristics:
- A business rule must be explained in such detail that it requires no further explanation
- Business rules should not be vague, they need to be specific.
- Business rules should have only one explanation that is not open to interpretation.
- Business rules should not be lengthy dissertations, but a single short sentence.
- Business rules should be documented within a policy and procedure framework.

Figure 28.1 identifies the information that is required when documenting business rules.

Name:	Returns goods receipts
Identifier:	GR123
Description:	No product returns will be accepted without a receipt. Each item returned must be accompanied by the original purchase receipt
Example:	none
Source:	Company Policies and Procedures Doc ID: GR701 Publication date: August 14, 2006
Related rules:	BR12 Supplying receipts
Owner	Head of Supply Chain

Figure 28.1

Value of business rules

A business rule provides rules for business processes. It stands to reason that if business rules are not developed and communicated then processes will be error prone and may take longer than required to execute. If employees are unsure of the returns rule for example, they may accept returns without receipts. Returns that are invalid, and are processed will affect an organization's inventory levels as well as sales revenues.

Without the clear definition and communication of business rules, employees will tend to make up their own rules.

Once business rules are formalized, it may be possible to imbed them in technologies to automate enforcement or compliance.

Benefits of defining business rules

- Allows for the clear separation of business rules from business processes.
- Provides for internal checks and balances that enable the enforcement of policies.
- Enabling processes to be executed without errors and delays.
- If business rules can be developed and embedded in Business Rules engines, an organization can move to flexible processes and Business Process Management (BPM).
- Support the consistent application of corporate business policies.
- Improve communication of key business concepts. Business rules are used to help the organization to better achieve goals, communicate among principals and agents, communicate between the organization and interested third parties, and demonstrate fulfillment of legal obligations.
- Allow for organization agility by enabling simple and rapid response to changing requirements, as it often easier to change a rule than a process.
- Lower cost to create or update the parts of applications that implement business policies.
- Allow management to easily audit the software services that implement their corresponding business rules and policies.

29. Policies

Policies are typically documented rules of acceptable conduct or rules of engagement within an organization. They are the official statement of an organization's business rules, and they are used to communicate behaviors that are allowed and not allowed. They are developed for the organization's employees and business partners, and are meant to communicate a business rule.

Policies are required to ensure a safe, organized, empowering, and nondiscriminatory work place. Policies should not be developed for every exception to accepted and expected behavior. Policy development is for the many employees, not for the few exceptions.

Reasons for developing policies

- To provide guidance about the most suitable way to handle various situations (standards of conduct, travel expenditures, purchase of company merchandise).
- To eliminate confusion in employees behavior. about the most appropriate way to behave (for example; dress codes, e-mail and internet policies, and cell phone use).
- To protect the company legally (consistent investigation of charges of harassment, non discriminatory hiring and promotion).
- To keep the company in compliance with governmental policies and laws such as minimum wage.
- To establish and document consistent work standards, rules, and regulations (progressive discipline, safety rules, break rules, smoking rules).
- To provide consistent and fair treatment for employees (benefits eligibility, paid time off, tuition assistance, bereavement time, jury duty).[11]

How to know what policies to develop

Policies should be developed for those business processes that have elements of variability that require approval, control, or oversight of some kind. Without formally developed and documented policies, organizations will exhibit the following characteristics:

- Employees and business partners will not understand their boundaries and what they are allowed and not allowed to do.
- Process activities and the completion of these activities will require constant supervision.
- Process activities will require constant revision or rework to conform to these undocumented policies.
- Processes will not be compliant with regulations and controls.

The Process Decomposition Model and Business Rules will provide ideas of what policies need to be developed.

- For each business process, identify if there is any constraining or explaining behavior required.
- For each of these behaviors identify if a communication is required to explain the behavior required.
- Develop a policy template (organization specific).
- Develop and document the policy in a clear and concise language. The policy example in figure 29.1 explains quite clearly what is the company's return policy. [12]
- Validate the policy for correctness by "expert" department heads.
- Validate, where appropriate, with legal, finance, and governance personnel.
- Communicate and publish these policies and make them accessible to employees.

Here is an example of a sales returns policy that clearly and thoroughly explains all relevant aspects to customers prior to returning goods.

```
┌─────────────────────────────────────────────────────────────┐
│                        THANK YOU                              │
│                                                               │
│  Thank you for purchasing our products. We proudly stand      │
│  behind everything we make and want you to be completely      │
│  satisfied with your order.                                   │
│                                                               │
│  If, however you find it necessary to return any part of      │
│  your shipment, for any reason, our return policy is as       │
│  follows:                                                     │
│                                                               │
│  • Any stock item may be returned for full credit within 3    │
│    weeks from shipment date.                                  │
│  • From 3 weeks to 60 days from shipment date a minimum       │
│    restocking charge of 15% will be made on all returns.      │
│  • No material will be accepted for return after 60 days!     │
│  • Shipping charges will not be refunded.                     │
│  • Special items, copies, repairs etc. are not returnable.    │
│    If you have a problem with any custom work, please call     │
│    for instructions.                                          │
│                                                               │
└─────────────────────────────────────────────────────────────┘
```

Figure 29.1

135

Notes and Action Items

30. Procedures

A procedure is a document that contains fixed, step-by-step actions that must be followed to perform a task correctly. Procedures are developed for employees, business partners, and customers.

A company cannot ask the customer to follow a work instruction. It can, however, ask customers to follow a procedure. Accordingly, a procedure is also the external manifestation of a work instruction. A procedure is required to explain how to conform to or follow a policy.

Standard Operating Procedures (SOPs) are a type of procedure. For the purpose of this process support element we will refer to procedures as SOPs. SOPs are an integral part of the Food and Drug Association (FDA) Good Manufacturing Practices (GMP). Regulated industries such as Life Sciences and Biotech commonly use SOPs in their daily routines. In fact most of the operations in these industries are done based on specific written procedures, commonly referred to as SOPs.

A Standard Operating Procedure is a written step-by-step procedure for an activity carried out in a particular organization. Quite simply, SOPs specify in writing:

What should be done,
When it should be done,
Where it should be done, and
Who should do it.

The FDA defines SOPs as written procedures that accurately describe and detail essential job tasks. For example, in 21 *CFR* 211.100, the regulation states: "There shall be written procedures for production and process control designed to assure that the drug products have the identity, strength, quality, and purity they purport or are represented to possess. Such procedures shall include all requirements in this subpart. These written procedures, including any changes, shall be drafted, reviewed, and approved by the appropriate organizational units and reviewed and approved by the quality control unit."

Steps to develop SOPs include:
- Develop the SOP for SOPs first. This SOP is mandatory.
- Follow the acronym SPICE when developing SOPs: SOPs must be practical, implementable, clear and effective.
- Develop a standard template for all SOPs. It must contain:
  - SOP Title
  - SOP number, and the date when the SOP was prepared or reviewed
  - Aim or Objective of the SOP
  - Scope of the SOP (area that will be covered by the SOP)
  - Procedures, processes, or steps to be carried out, in sequential order
  - Responsibilities
  - References
  - Safety Instructions
  - Name and signature of the person or persons who developed or reviewed the SOPs, along with date of review
  - Any other useful information or appendices

The benefits of developing SOPs are:
- Provides clarity on how to perform certain job activities.
- Eliminates or reduces errors as procedures provide directions to enable a consistent method for getting a task completed.
- SOPs assist to ensure that GMP's are followed and achieved at all times.
- SOPs are useful tools for training new members of staff.

31. Integrating Business Rules, Policies, and Procedures

Business processes, business rules, policies, and procedures are often confused with each other. It thus makes sense to show how the process support elements interact with each other.

Firstly, there is a business process that defines a particular set of actions to perform a task, such as processing a returns receipt.

Secondly, there are business rules that define conditions that guide the execution of a business process. In a returns example, a rule would identify under what condition a return can be executed.

Thirdly, rules are communicated to employees, customers and business partners via a policy. The returns rule above will be documented in a formal policy and communicated to customers, often via the company website.

Lastly, procedures are developed to explain how to comply with the business process and business rules. Procedures include the documented steps that explain how to perform an activity defined in a policy statement. Using the returns example, a procedure will detail the steps a customer must follow to return the goods to the organization. Figure 31.1 provides an example of how business rules, policies, and procedures are inter-related.

Business Process:

The business process shows the steps to execute the process. The "Confirm dates on return slip" activity will either be a manual activity executed by a goods receiver, or an automated check in the returns transaction of a computer system. This automated check will have the business rule codified in a program that will do the date check.

Business Rule:

The business rule clearly states the return policy of the company.

Policy:

The rule is explained in clear, understandable language in the form of a policy.

Procedure:

The Procedure communicates how to execute the policy. It provides customers the list of actions they must take so that the goods can be returned.

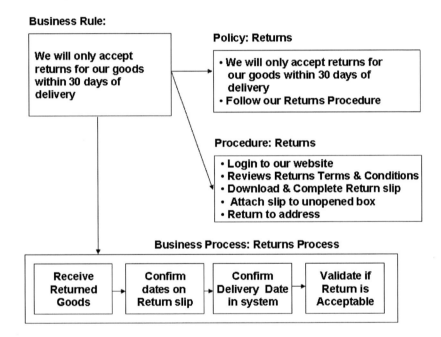

Business Rule:

We will only accept returns for our goods within 30 days of delivery

Policy: Returns

• We will only accept returns for our goods within 30 days of delivery
• Follow our Returns Procedure

Procedure: Returns

• Login to our website
• Reviews Returns Terms & Conditions
• Download & Complete Return slip
• Attach slip to unopened box
• Return to address

Business Process: Returns Process

| Receive Returned Goods | Confirm dates on Return slip | Confirm Delivery Date in system | Validate if Return is Acceptable |

Figure 31.1

32. Work Instructions

A work instruction is a document showing the detailed sequence of steps or activities that an employee needs to follow each time he or she performs a task. Work instructions are sometimes referred to as Standard Operating Procedures (SOPs) or procedures. They define and document the "how" to do work. This is arguably the most important element of the business process ecosystem.

There are several reasons for developing work instructions. The purpose of a work instruction is to organize steps in a logical format so that an employee can easily follow it. A key reason for developing work instructions is to provide employees with a documented process so the operator/worker does not have to remember the specifics of the process.

Once training is completed, documented work instructions and procedures are what most employees depend on to help them with executing their tasks.

There is no perfect format for work instructions. Most organizations develop their own standard template. Below are some ideas for a template:

- Develop this at Level 5 or Level 6 of the decomposition model.
- Develop a work instruction template and define standards (font, content, etc).
- Test the work instructions out during the delivery of end user training and refine accordingly.

A work instruction should contain at a minimum the following:

- Description
- Steps to execute the tasks
- Screen shots of system transactions
- Data Standards for data to be entered into the system transactions

The benefits of developing work instructions include:

- Provides employees the detail information they require to perform a job function.
- Improves business process execution time as there are no "time wasters" of employees searching or asking how to perform a certain task.
- Eliminates or reduces errors as work instructions provide a consistent method for getting a task completed.
- Can be used as a training tool for new employees.

33. Systems Transactions

Activities in a business process can either be executed manually or via a system. System transactions in the context of the business process ecosystem are the detailed documentation that provides a user guidance to execute a transaction and what data to enter into the different screens and fields. System transactions are typically found documented as part of a work instruction.

Steps for developing system transactions

- Identify the systems transactions required to support the Level 6 processes in the process decomposition model.
- Print screen shots of each transaction.
- Identify all data elements on the screens that require data to be input into the screen.
- Document the content for each data element and what value an end user needs to enter into the system transaction.

To facilitate the ease of use of the system, the system transaction should have a description of each of the data elements that need to be populated. For example:

Order Type:
- o Enter NB for standard orders
- o Enter UB for transport orders

Purchasing Group:
- o Enter 003 for HQ

Location of Plant:
- o Enter 004 for PA plant
- o Enter 005 for NJ plant

Figure 33.1 is an example of an IT system transaction. This figure is a screen shot of the Create Purchase Order transaction found in the SAP ERP system.

Create Purchase Order: Initial Screen

Copy Requisition

Order Type	NB
Purchase Order Date	12/30/2009
Purchasing Group	003
Source Determination	

Default data for items
Item Category	
Acct Assignment Cat.	
Delivery Date	T
Plant	
Storage Location	
Material Group	
Req. Tracking Number	

Figure 33.1

Employees need to be trained to use the system transaction. If employees do not understand how to use these transactions, then transactions may be completed incorrectly; errors will be made and will need to be corrected later in the process. In addition, transactions may not be complete; this will also result in rework.

Both of the above instances will cause sub-optimal performance of a business process and can lead to a crisis in the business, such as a purchase order for a critical item not being placed on the Vendor at the correct time.

Benefits of developing system transactions

- Reduces errors and rework as employees can reference "How to Complete a Transaction" documentation.
- Allows for optimum processing execution as employees' time is not spent asking, "What do I enter in this field?"
- Facilitates consistent usage of system transactions.
- Reduces or eliminates errors and thus reduces rework.
- Enables processes to be executed quicker.
- Can be used to train new employees on how to execute system transactions.

Notes and Action Items

34. Data Standards

A data standard can be defined as a set of rules that describes how data is formatted, presented, used, exchanged, and stored. The data standard will also describe the definition and format of a data attribute or field.

There is no such thing as a good, efficient, effective business process with bad data. Business processes—and the data they use, manipulate, or create—cannot be decoupled from each other. For a company to have good business processes, it needs to have good data. Developing data standards is the first step toward having good data. A Data Standard should contain the following information:

- Data element. This should conform to a predefined naming convention. This refers to the accepted identifier of the data element.
- Data element description
- Data standard
- Naming Convention. Data Structure. This refers to the length of the data element (number of characters) and the format. For example MM.DD.YYYY for a data element called Sales Order Received Date.
- Data Values. This refers to the prescribed data values for a data element. If we use a data element called Sales Organization for example, its prescribed values could be:

  NE – for the North East Sales Organization
  MW – for the Mid West Sales Organization
  WC – for the West Coast Sales Organization.

- Data structure
- Data values
- Owner of the data element
- Who is authorized to change the data element

Data standards facilitate the development, sharing, and use of data. These standards also enable the common usage of data within an organization's application systems. Data standards also facilitate consistent usage of system transactions. Consistent use of good data standards will reduce or eliminate errors and thus reduces rework. Strong data standards enable processes to be executed quicker.

An example of a Data Standard for the data element, Customer Number, is described as:

- Data Values will be in the number range 1000000 to 3000000
- The Naming Convention will be Customer Number – not Customer No, not Customer #, not Cust Number; not Cust Numb.
- Data Structure will be eight numeric characters, and no alpha numeric characters.

Figure 34.1 is a view of the Create Material transaction in the SAP ERP System.

Figure 34.1

Data standards need to be defined and documented for data elements such as:

- Material number
- Material description
- Unit of measure.

Notes and Action Items

35. Process and Compliance Controls

Process and compliance controls are sometimes referred to as business controls, financial controls, process controls, management controls, or internal controls as defined by The Committee of Sponsoring Organizations (COSO).

A multilevel control environment consists of three elements: strategic, management, and process controls: [14]

Strategic controls

Strategic controls refer to those activities within the strategic management process that help management to understand the effect of external and internal factors on the business and strategy. Strategic controls define the environment of risk and control behavior and align the organization with these strategies.

Management controls

Management controls are those activities and elements that must be present in the control system throughout the organization if it is to identify, assess, and react to business risks and attain its objectives. These controls develop from the results of environmental reviews performed during the strategic planning process.

Process controls

Process controls are the control activities performed at the process, or function, level. They are normally the responsibilities of process, or functional, owners who ensure that the control activities are in place and meet their objectives. In the process of managing or serving collections, for example, the process owner would be a collection custodian.

Large, complex organizations have literally thousands of controls that are managed by potentially many employees. This underscores the importance of ensuring that the organization has the right controls at the right points in its processes.

It is also important to not create too many controls, or controls that do not support the organization's objectives. As stated earlier controls are meant to provide assurance of meeting objectives, controls are not meant to drive bureaucracy.

In the context of the BPE, we will focus on the development of process controls. Process controls can be described as:

- Behaviors you want to prevent
- Behaviors you want to encourage or enforce
- Behaviors you want to manage
- Behaviors you want to track

The framework used to develop controls is:

- Define control objectives.
- Identify control actions that will assist or must be in place to meet or satisfy the control objective.
- Identify control tasks that need to be performed (in a system, process or document) that will enable to control action.

Figure 35.1 shows the steps involved in identifying and creating process controls.

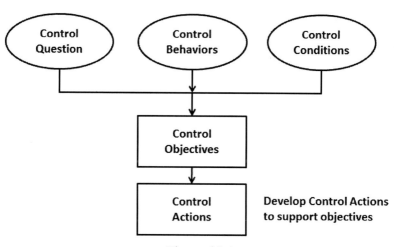

Developing Controls

Figure 35.1

It's sometimes difficult to define Control Objectives. Asking control questions can assist in identifying controls and developing control objectives. A control is developed as a control objective.

For each process, ask and list control questions both from a management perspective and an operational perspective. Doing this activity will help you identify control objectives. A question could be: "Do we want anyone to be able to create a purchase order?"

Define one or more control objectives in clear unambiguous language. An example is "prevent unauthorized creation of purchase orders." To assist in this activity, determine:

- What behavior needs to be enforced?
- What behavior needs to be prevented?

Identify control actions necessary to meet the control objectives. As an example a control action is: "limit the creation of purchase orders to the procurement department only."

Validate that the control actions are complete by reviewing conditions and asking:

- What conditions must be in place before the process is executed?

- What conditions need to be in place after the process is executed?

The following example uses a Sales Order Process to ask all the relevant control questions, develop control objectives, and define control actions. The process has the following four activities:

- Receive purchase order from customer
- Enter purchase order in system as a sales order
- Pick, pack, and ship the goods to the customer
- Send the customer an invoice

To assist in the identification of Control Objectives we ask the following questions:

- How can we ensure we charge customers correctly?
- How can we ensure that the customer gets the correct product and the correct quantity they ordered?
- How can we ensure that the customer is charged the correct price for the product?

The Control Objectives we develop from the questions are:

- Invoices are accurately calculated and recorded.
- Ship the correct products to customers
- Track that customers receive the correct goods they ordered.
- Ensure the price we charge the customer is the price we quoted.

To assist in the definition of control objectives we review some behaviors that should be enforced:

- Only pre approved customers are allowed to buy.
- Enforce that only valid orders are entered into the system.

We also review some behaviors that should be prevented:

- If customers are in arrears with their payments, they will not be allowed to place orders.
- Defective products should not be sold to customers. Saleable products should therefore have a "sellable" disposition.

The list of Control Objectives is enhanced by adding additional objectives:
- All orders received from customers are input and processed.
- Only valid orders are input and processed.

The Control Actions we develop for the control objectives are:
- Confirm delivery against sales order (quantity and correct item)
- Confirm quoted prices, order price and invoice price are consistent.

To assist in the definition of control actions we review some conditions that are necessary to meet the objectives and actions.

What conditions should be in place before the process is executed?
- All customers must have a contract set up in the system.
- All products must be set up in a product catalog.

What conditions should be in place after the process is executed?
- Documentation should match the actual results (e.g., invoice, pick slip).
- The picking slip in the warehouse should match the delivery note.
- The invoice should match the delivery note.
- The computer systems should reflect actual results:
  o Sales revenue figures increase with the value of the sale.
  o Inventory levels reduce by the quantity of product bought.
- There should be verification that the goods have been shipped to the customer.

The final task in the development of control objectives is to define tasks that must be completed so the control actions can be enforced.

Figure 35.2 is an example of controls for the sales order process, with their corresponding control actions.

Process	Control Objective	Control Action	Control Task
Deliver goods and services	Only preapproved customers can buy from us	Sales Orders must have valid customer number	Configure Sales Orders to require a customer number
		New customer requests must satisfy all approvals	Ensure New customer requests have approvals activities
Deliver goods and services	We will only sell standard products	Sales to be trained	Train Sales
		Manufacturing to be notified	Develop a communication to mfg.
Deliver goods and services	Customers in arrears cannot be allowed to place new orders	Sales Order process to check customer payment status	Configure sales orders to check customer payment status and disallow processing
Deliver goods and services	Defective products must not be sold to customers	Only product that has passed QA to have saleable status	Process to include a QA step
		Sales orders to check product status	Inventory dispositions to be defined

Figure 35.2

Benefits of developing process controls include:

- Developing controls in this manner provides a level of diligence that reveals opportunities for business improvements.
- Improves the performance of a business, as management should use the controls to manage the business.
- Provide improved transparency for business management.
- Properly defined and documented control objectives and control actions assist with making audits easier.
- Improves the definition of controls across the organization, including the crucial relationship between these controls and risk.
- Can reduce the risk of fraud and can enforce the compliance of regulations.
- Improves process and business efficiency [10]

36. Metrics

Metrics and Key Performance Indicators (KPI's) are often used interchangeably and confused with each other. Let's explore the definitions of each.

A metric is a standard of measurement by which efficiency, performance, progress, or quality of a plan, process, or product can be assessed. They are established to measure a business's progress in measurable terms.

KPIs are quantifiable metrics which reflect the performance of an organization in achieving its goals and objectives. KPIs reflect strategic value drivers rather than just measuring non-critical business activities and processes. It is important to bear in mind that although all KPIs are metrics, not all metrics are KPIs.

Defining metrics or KPIs for an organization is not a trivial task. Metrics or KPIs are often developed during a separate project. For this exercise assume that the organization's overall measurement objectives have already been decided, and that the only task at hand is to identify and develop metrics.

The key requirements for identifying KPIs are predefined business processes, and clear goals and performance requirements for the selected business processes.

Below is a checklist and an example of activities required to develop metrics:

- Write down what you want to measure. This sounds fairly trivial, but it provides a good starting point to develop a measure. Simply put down, in writing, what you want to measure.
- Define the purpose of the data collection. There should always be a reason why we are collecting the data. Write down the purpose of the data collection.
- Determine if other measures are appropriate for the processes involved. Look at the processes from the dimensions of quality, quantity, timeliness, and cost.

- Define what attribute you want to measure, below are examples of measurement attributes:

  Effectiveness:
  - How close to requirements does the product or output conform?
  - Are you doing the right things?

  Efficiency:
  - How efficient does the process produce the output?
  - Are you doing things right?

  Quality:
  - Does the output meet quality expectations?

  Timeliness:
  - Is the output delivered according to agreed standards?

  Productivity:
  - How productive is the process?
  - Is value added?

- Determine if the measurement is currently being taken and if there is historical data available. If the measurement is currently being taken, the process becomes easier since people are already taking the data.
- Determine who will collect the data. A decision must be made about who should collect the data. It is usually best if the person closest to the process collect the data.
- Determine how the data will be collected and how it will be displayed. This is a crucial step. If the process for defining how the data will be collected is not correct, a lot of time and effort can be wasted. Questions to consider include:
  - Can the data be automatically collected?
  - Can the data be downloaded from the system?
  - Will the data have to be manually collected?
  - Can the data be collected from reports?
  - Should the data be displayed as a control chart or a Pareto diagram?
  - What steps do I expect the data collectors to go through to

collect the data?
- Determine how to ensure the data collection process takes place. Develop a series of controls to ensure the data is collected, reported, and acted upon.
- Determine who will review the data and how often. We collect data too often for the sake of collecting data. We don't review the data and no action is taken on it.

Once you have identified and created a measure or metric, you should validate that it makes sense. The acronym SMART is often applied to the process of developing KPIs. Review the SMART items below to ensure your metric definition is complete.

Specific
- Is it specific and targeted to the area that is being measured?

Measurable
- Are you able to collect the required data to enable measurement?

Actionable
- Is it easy to understand?
- Do you understand which direction is "good" and which direction is "bad," so that you know when to take action?

Relevant
- Measuring only what is relevant and important

Timely
- Getting the data in a timely matter to make measurement relevant

Implement the process. You have planned it. Now go do it. Often you will need to make revisions to the process once it has been implemented to help improve the quality of the data collection.

Things to remember:
- KPIs should not be developed in isolation, but within an integrated framework that includes Business Intelligence, reporting and data.

- Develop metrics to measure end-to-end processes.
- Don't develop too many metrics, this will make the exercise meaningless.
- An organization needs to develop processes to perform corrective actions if, for example, a process under-performs and shows declining performance.
- Remember that defining KPIs is not a onetime effort; an organization must set up processes to monitor KPIs and not just report on them.
- Develop metrics from the customer perspective; too often metrics are too internally focused and not customer focused.

Below are some metrics as per the SCOR model from the SCC. These metrics are defined at the business process level (Level 3). The formulas for each metric are also supplied with the SCOR model.

- Perfect order fulfillment
- Responsiveness source cycle time
- Flexibility upside source flexibility
- Downside source adaptability
- Upside source adaptability
- Cost product acquisition costs as a percentage of source (S1) costs
- Assets cash to cash cycle time
- Return on supply chain fixed assets.

The reasons and benefits of developing metrics include:

- It has been well-documented in management literature that "what is not measured is not managed," developing metrics allows an organization to measure its health, performance and effectiveness.
- It is impossible to measure the benefits of process improvement initiatives without the existence of metrics data.
- KPIs align all levels of an organization (business units, departments and individuals) with clearly defined and cascaded targets and benchmarks to create accountability and track progress.

- KPIs accelerate seamless and collaborative planning across the organization to ensure that everyone is operating from the same playbook.
- Provides clear goals to an organization on how it is going to measure business performance.
- Provides an idea of what is important to management.
- Provides performance targets for management.
- Provides data for process improvement initiatives.

Metrics can be documented in a number of ways. Figure 36.1 is a template used to document metrics.

Performance Meas. Title:	Open Item List		
Process (level 1)	Deliver Products and Services	Process (level 2)	Procure Materials and Services
Process (level 3)	Verify Invoices		
Performance Meas. Type:	Business Metric – Time, Quality, Cost		

Performance Measurement Description:

The intent of this metric is to measure the number of documents that are due for payment and the aging of those documents. This will aide in identifying the average daily payables and any cash flow requirements. It will also determine those that are past due and trigger the user to investigate any blocked/parked items.

Method of Measurement:

Invoice date vs. Due date

Data Sources:	Frequency:
Aged open item list	Daily
Metric Owner:	Jim

Figure 36.1

161

Notes and Action Items

37. Reports, Interfaces, Conversions, Extensions, and Forms

Reports, interfaces, conversions, extensions, and forms (RICEF) are objects that are inputs to business processes, or outputs of business processes, or used during the execution of business processes. It is thus important to have these RICEF objects documented.

Reports: Many business processes are either supported by reports, or they produce a report as an output to the process.

Interfaces: Interfaces and Electronic Data Interchange (EDI) transactions send data from one computer system to another. This is often used to facilitate further processing or reporting.

Conversions: Refer to data conversion programs that are developed during projects to perform initial data loads of a system.

Extensions: Are the modifications and add-ons done to existing system programs to enhance their functionality.

Forms: Are documents such as purchase orders and invoices.

RICEF elements are typically initially developed during ERP and IT system implementations, and are continuously developed and modified as business needs change:

- RICEF elements are part of a business process and are either used as inputs into a process, or produced as an output of a process.
- RICEF elements can also be integration points between external parties or internal departments.
- RICEF development typically follows the following process:
- RICEF objects are typically identified when a technology solution is framed to support a business problem or requirement.
- Each RICEF object identified must be validated as necessary and

a true requirement.
- Functional specifications are developed, by the business, to document the business requirement.
- Technical specifications are developed by IT, using the functional specifications as a basis.
- Programming efforts are mobilized to develop the code.
- Testing occurs to ensure that it works.
- Sign-off occurs to ensure the requirements have been met.

An organization needs to develop and document RICEF elements as they are either inputs or outputs of business processes.

38. Knowledge Management

Knowledge management is the name of a discipline in which an enterprise gathers, organizes, shares, and analyzes its knowledge in terms of resources, documents, experiences, and people skills.

Knowledge management is the process through which organizations generate value from their intellectual and knowledge-based assets by the reuse and sharing of these assets. It is the codifying of organizational learning by collecting what employees, partners, and customers know and sharing that information among employees.

From a business process perspective, knowledge management can accelerate the performance of business processes by supplying relevant data or information to employees executing the processes. An example of this could be an IT help desk that has collected and categorized previous help desk requests, then makes this information available to help desk personnel so they can quickly respond to similar support requests.

The steps involved in developing knowledge management capabilities are specific to the kinds of intellectual property an organization wants to capture. The steps include:

- Identify what information or learning needs to be captured.
- Develop a template to gather the learning.
- Facilitate the capture and categorization of this learning.
- Implement a technology solution to store the learning captured.
- Make this learning ready available to resources who need it.
- Develop processes to maintain this knowledge and keep it current.

Institutionalizing organizational learning and making it possible to retrieve and access this learning, in such a manner that it helps other employees in the execution of their business processes, enables process excellence.

The main objective of knowledge management is to ensure that the *right* information is delivered to the *right* person at the *right* time, in order to make the most appropriate decision.

Notes and Action Items

39. Benefits of Developing Business Process Support Elements

Improved Management of the Business

For a process to be effectively managed and controlled, management needs to know how they can monitor the number of Returns as well as the different reasons for the Returns. Key Performance Indicators (KPIs) or Metrics need to be selected, the relevant data needs to be captured, and reports or dashboards need to be developed to report the process measurements.

Managers of the Receiving Department need reports to allow them to manage. They need to understand what reports to use, and how to analyze and use the reports. Reports are a Business Process Support Element.

To know if the process is secure or controlled, process controls need to be identified and put in place. An example of a process control is to not allow employees who process fraud claims to process customer payments. In this instance the process control will be enforced through systems security authorizations.

Developing BPSE allows an organization to be agile. An organization can adapt to changing conditions effectively if it knows what it does, and also knows how changes in the business impact the organization's processes and Business Process Support Elements.

Management will be able to answer the following questions:

- Are our business processes complete?
- Do we have all the necessary process controls in place?
- Are the processes secure?

Improved Operations

It is important to develop Business Process Support Elements because, without these being defined and communicated, a process will never be performed to its optimum potential. In the Returns Example, if the Business Process Support Elements were not developed and enforced, then the process would be unclear and vague, and returns could be executed for incorrect products.

It is clear that if Business Process Support Elements are not developed, there will be confusion as to what to do:

- Customers will not know how to return goods or under what conditions they may return goods.
- Employees who process returns will not know what goods they may receive, and may not even know how to process a return.

This confusion will result in increased time to process returns as well as potential errors, because employees:

- Are not trained and therefore make mistakes
- Do not understand policies and need to ask what to do
- Do not understand the rules and need to ask what to do
- Do not understand how to use system transactions, and what data to enter into certain fields

The development of Business Process Support Elements will reduce or eliminate the following questions from employees:

- What is my job?
- What do I do now?
- How do I do it?

Support elements increase the execution capability of an organization, because all the necessary elements are present to ensure a process is executed effectively and correctly.

Improved Quality of Business Process Initiatives

The Business Process Support Elements provide all the elements that are necessary for the successful execution and management of business processes. Business processes will be incomplete without these support elements.

Organization Mindset

The Business Process Ecosystem will assist in moving an organization to a process mindset:

- Processes will be described as processes instead of functions.
- Processes will be identified in the Model.
- Business Process Support Elements will be developed to improve the execution of business processes.
- Metrics and Reporting will provide the organization the information needed to manage and optimize the business processes.

Business Process Development

The Business Process Ecosystem provides the ability to scope a business process project. All business processes and process support elements can be identified.

Developing a decomposition model will enable the identification of all business processes.

The Business Process Ecosystem will allow for the identification of all work and deliverables to be developed. This will provide a view to management or project sponsors of what done looks like, with a clear definition of deliverables.

Business Process Execution in Operations

The Business Process Ecosystem provides tools to enable employees to execute processes flawlessly (access to all process ecosystem documentation).

Process execution will be improved as all users will have the required policies, business rules, procedures, and work instructions available to them. This will reduce or prevent processing errors.

Business Process Support and Maintenance

The Business Process Ecosystem provides tools to enable the support of business and IT solutions.

Business Process Optimization Initiatives

The Business Process Decomposition Model is a tool that facilitates business process optimization as it can be used to identify business process improvement opportunities as it provides the ability to show dependencies and integration points between multiple processes.

Business Process Optimization initiatives can also be improved if a sound process baseline is established. This baseline is the decomposition model.

Communication

Business communication is improved as the business processes and their support documentation can be made available to the organization.

Summary

The above list of business process support elements is by no means exhaustive. One could argue Workflow and Web Services are also process support elements. An organization can define and develop process support elements as it sees fit.

40. From Theory to Practice

There are three options or paths to developing a business process ecosystem:

1. *Initiate a process documentation initiative.* This is initiating a project to specifically develop and document the process ecosystem for the business.
2. *Develop the process ecosystem as part of a systems project.* This is developing and documenting the ecosystem process by process. It is about defining standards and then ensuring these standards are followed.
3. *Develop the process ecosystem as part of a process project.* This is initiating a project to specifically develop and document the process ecosystem for the business. This is done during a business process improvement initiative or a BPM initiative.

The first thing to do is to stop the bleeding, and put processes and standards in place to enforce process documentation. The IT department will be the drivers and enforcers of this. Steps to achieve moving from theory to practice are:

- Define and document process documentation standards.
- Communicate the standards to project and process teams.
- Initiate a process to ensure that each project develops process documentation, and that it follows the prescribed standards.
- Check and validate that the process documentation is complete and that it follows the prescribed standards.

Sounds like a lot of hard work? Indeed it is. But there's never been anything easy about business. Furthermore, developing a business process ecosystem is not an event—it's a journey. I wish you great success in your journey ahead.

INDEX

References

[1] Mark McGregor – The real motivation behind BPM

A BPT Column 2004

[2] Michael Hammer

[3] Roger Maull, Director of the Exeter University Centre for Research in Strategic Processes & Operations

[4] *Extreme Competition*, Peter Fingar

[5] *Balanced Scorecard & Strategy Maps* - Norton & Kaplan

[6] Excerpts from: Porter, Michael E., Harvard Business Review, Nov/Dec96, Vol. 74 , Issue 6, p61

[7] The Supply Chain Council has developed the Supply Chain Operations Reference Model (SCOR)

[8] Telemanagement Forum (tmforum)

[9] APQC, Association Production Quality Control

[10] Microsoft Corporation; Regulatory Compliance Planning Guide.

Section 1: IT Controls Published: June 14, 2006

[11] Susan M Heathfield (About.com) Human Resources – How to develop a policy

[12] Bell and Bell

[13] Information Technology Infrastructure Library

[14] *Managing Cultural Assets from a Business Perspective*, Laura Price and Abby Smith, March 2000

About the Author

Arthur C. Harris is an internationally experienced management and business process consultant who has worked for companies such as Robert Bosch, DuPont, Deloitte & Touche, and CIBER, and he is currently a business transformation consultant at SAP. Selected companies Arthur has consulted to include Caterpillar, Harley-Davidson, Colgate, Sanofi Aventis, Medicis, and Samsung.

Arthur is a member of the Association of Business Process Management Professionals and also regularly presents at Business Process forums. He is an adjunct professor at Widener University School of Business where he teaches Business Process Management.

Companion Books at www.mkpress.com

www.mkpress.com/Cloud

"My experience in building complex distributed systems and Cloud Computing platforms provides me a detailed view of how these types of systems are assembled, used by developers, and will likely evolve. However, I felt that I was missing the cloud (forest) for the technical details (trees). I was lacking a larger vision of how companies, markets and consumption could change as Cloud Computing evolves. I turned to Peter Fingar's *Dot.Cloud* book to see if he could provide a vision for these areas. Just as in Alvin Tofler's *Future Shock*, Dot.Cloud paints a challenging vision of what may change due to Cloud Computing. Using Peter Schwartz' (*Art of the Long View*) notion of accepting what could happen, I found Fingar's book eye-opening." —Mark Hodapp, Cloudsavvy

A Strategy Guide For
Business and Technology Leaders

ENTERPRISE
CLOUD
COMPUTING

Andy Mulholland
Jon Pyke and Peter Fingar

www.mkpress.com/ECC

No one needs to know more about the business implications of Cloud Computing than C-level executives responsible for the future of their companies, for the wow isn't just about technology, it's about the promise of on-demand business innovation. But even more than understanding this new wave, they need to act, and act now.

Written by industry veterans with a combined leadership experience of over 100 years at the intersection of business and technology, *Enterprise Cloud Computing* provides strategic insights, describes the breakout business models, and offers the planning and implementation guidance business and technology leaders need to chart their course ahead.

Cloud Brokers
Business Architecture
Deliberatorium
Innovation Economy
TRIZ
Cognitive Computer
Business Agility
Social Networks
Human Interaction Management
Open Leadership
Business Insights
Multi-Agent Systems
Services Avatars
Argumentation Systems
Collective Intelligence
Fractal Company

Listening Posts
Surface Computing
Affective Computing
Mobility

Next-Generation CIO
Unified Communications
Persona Management Systems
Open Innovation

Business Innovation in the Cloud

Bioteams
Big Data   Weak Ties
Intercloud

Energy Maneuverability
End of Management
Augmented Reality
Cloud Computing Capitalism 3.0
Predictive Analytics Strong Ties
Shared Value
Sentiment Analysis
Process Innovation

OODA Loops
IT Services
Services Innovation

Executing on Innovation with Cloud Computing

Jim Stikeleather | Peter Fingar

Foreword by
Derek Miers
Forrester Research

"This exciting and deeply insightful book offers a compelling vision of how the Cloud will rewrite the rules of business."
Gary Hamel
London Business School, Author of *What Matters Now*

www.mkpress.com/BIC

"This exciting and deeply insightful book offers a compelling vision of how the Cloud will rewrite the rules of business."
—Gary Hamel, London Business School,
Author of What Matters Now

SAMURAI BUSINESS

The way of the warrior
for professionals
in the digital century

By Joris Merks
Research Manager Google
and
European Champion Brazilian Jiu-Jitsu

Artwork by Thera Benjaminsen

www.mkpress.com/SB

The digital age of *transparency* has imposed changes on businesses that make the Samurai teachings of self-discipline a valuable resource. Companies relying on power, control or low ethical standards, are losing ground. More than ever, success comes from a purpose beyond earning money. Success must be based on *integrity*, but how can we cherish integrity while facing fierce competition and company/office politics?

The path of the Samurai is a quest for self-development that extends beyond fighting. The Samurai became successful in battle through true skill and the ability to withstand the desire for power and victory. *Integrity* is not naivety, and kindness does not equal weakness.

It is time to put the *self-discipline of the Samurai in the professional.*

www.mkpress.com/bio

Bioteams is a handbook for a new business model in which ideas are no longer developed behind closed doors, but across company boundaries and amongst diverse groups of people. It is this spirit of collaboration, not competition that will be critical if we are to address the major social and economic challenges that lie ahead.

—Jonathan Kestenbaum, CEO, The National Endowment for Science, Technology and the Arts and Board member of the Design Council, the UK Technology Strategy Board and the Royal Shakespeare Company

EXTREME COMPETITION

INNOVATION AND THE GREAT 21ST CENTURY BUSINESS REFORMATION

PETER FINGAR

www.mkpress.com/extreme

Watch for forthcoming titles.

Meghan-Kiffer Press

Tampa, Florida, USA

www.mkpress.com

Advanced Business-Technology Books for Competitive Advantage